FORCED OUT OF VIETNAM

A POLICY ANALYSIS OF THE FALL OF SAIGON

BY

BEN WOOD JOHNSON

EDUKA SOLUTIONS & TESKO PUBLISHING

Forced Out Of Vietnam: A Policy Analysis Of The Fall Of Saigon

ES & TKP

EDUKA SOLUTIONS & TESKO PUBLISHING

Cover Design by Wood Oliver

Published in the United States by Eduka solutions & Tesko Publishing, 2017
Ben Wood Johnson

Forced Out Of Vietnam: A Policy Analysis Of The Fall Of Saigon
Includes bibliographical references (p.)
1. National security—United States of America. 2. United States—Military policy. 3. United States—Foreign policy. 4. United States—War policy.

ISBN-10: 0-9979028-6-8
ISBN-13: 978-0-9979028-6-0
Format: Paperback

≈≈≈≈≈

FORCED OUT OF VIETNAM

A POLICY ANALYSIS OF THE FALL OF SAIGON

FIRST EDITION

BEN WOOD JOHNSON

Eduka Solutions & Tesko Publishing
Middletown, PA

"Your mind is your weapon for survival; your thoughts are your ammos."

B.W.J.
March 22, 2017

Contents

Preface   *xi*

A Class Assignment   *xiii*

The Book Project   *xv*

Acknowledgments   *xix*

Introduction   *1*

I. THE VIETNAM CULPRIT
BLAMING CONGRESS

1. A Treacherous War 7

2. Mixed Views About Congress 17

II. A WAR OF PRIDE
NOT AMERICA'S WAR

3. A Military Graveyard 25

4. The First Vietnam War 33

5. The Second Vietnam War 37

II. A TOUGH WAR
VIETNAM AND MILITARY HISTORY

6. A Complex Military Conflict 47

7. Long-Term Effects Of The War 57

8. Vietnam As A Litmus Test 65

IV. THE POLITICS OF WAR
MANUFACTURING THE VIETNAM WAR

9. Political Support For Vietnam 73

10. Popular Writings About Vietnam 77

11. Leaving Vietnam 83

12. Examining War-Exit Strategies 91

V. <u>THE WITHDRAWAL DECISION</u>
THE ALLISON APPROACH

13. A Scientific Approach 101
14. A Change Of Direction 109
15. Applying The Models 117
16. Politics And Policy Making 125

<u>FINAL WORDS</u>
CONCLUSION & MISCELLANEOUS

Final Words 133
Notes 139
About The Author 153
Bibliography 155
Index 169
Dear Reader 185
Contact The Author 186
   Mailing/Postal Info: 186
   Phone: 186
   Electronic Address: 186

PREFACE

WHAT MAKES ME qualify to write about the Vietnam War? I am not a Vietnam War veteran. I do not have a military background. I do not even have any relative or close friend who experienced the conflict directly or vicariously. Understandably, I am not sure how to answer the above question with a convincing tone.

Nevertheless, one way I could put it is that certain aspects of the war fall within the realm of my academic interests. Although I do not have a real world experience[1] in policymaking, I do have the necessary background and the academic expertise to navigate the issues I will discuss in this document. Writing a book about Vietnam gives me the opportunity to share my views about the conflict. It is a rare occasion to explore an important event in human history.

I would also say that I chose to write about Vietnam because the effects of this military clash are still resounding in world affairs. Since the 1970s, every foreign military action envisioned or taken by the United States seems to revert to the Vietnam debacle. There is a genuine concern (at the domestic level of course) to avoid a repeat of the mistakes of the past, notably the monumental errors American officials seemingly made in Indochina.

To this day, any kinds of military actions (on a global scale of course) instigated by the United States, whether directly or else, often generate a staunch scrutiny. The common understanding is that it is always best to tread with caution, when it comes to international conflict. The idea is to avoid another Vietnam at all costs.

Truth be told; this was not always the case. But Vietnam changed everything. The effects of the war continue to reverberate in American foreign affairs. Vietnam is still a pertinent issue abroad. The remnants of this military skirmish are still palpable at home. For many commentators, Vietnam has become a curse in American politics.

Despite the fact that I propose to examine the Vietnam fiasco in the present work, I do not poise myself as an authority—or I could not pretend to be an expert—on the subject. As the war winded down, I came into this world.[2] Most of the data I gathered about Vietnam came from books, magazines, and articles I red many years after the conflict ended.

What I am saying here is that I did not experience Vietnam personally. My visual sense of what occurred in Indochina came from video footages and other graphic images, which I only had the chance to review [superficially of course] several decades after the fact. For these reasons, I could not characterize myself as an authority about Vietnam in any way, shape, or form.

That being adumbrated, this work proffers a glimpse into the underlying factors that led to the political rift, which, in turn, appeared conducive to the premature end of the conflict. In this regard, I hope to offer the reader the necessary insight so that he or she could make sense of Vietnam. I also hope that after reading this paperback, the reader would be able to decipher the reason the United States withdrew completely from Indochina in the spring of 1975.

Ben Wood Johnson, Ph.D.
April 12, 2017

A CLASS ASSIGNMENT

THIS BOOK STARTED as a class project.[1] I penned the initial words for this text while attending a graduate level course about American Government and Policy.[2] For many years, issues pertaining to world politics have been among my academic interests.

The course focused on American foreign affairs. It was a very interactive learning environment. The course was very popular on campus.[3] It examined American public policy from a very broad perspective. It also assessed the relationship between branches of government. But because it was a relatively short session, the course only explored two branches, in this instance, the Executive Branch and the Legislature.

In order to complete the course, students were required to research an event in American history. The event must have taken place between the 1950s and the 1970s. The topic was supposed to address a governmental decision, which had a great impact on American foreign policy initiatives.

The event must have also had an influence on the country as a whole. I must admit it; I was seeking an easy topic to explore. I was nearing the end of the program and I could not wait any longer to graduate.

I decided to examine the Vietnam War. Due to the popularity of this event, I thought I would be able to cruise through to subject with breeze. But as I immersed myself in the assignment, I found out that the issues were more complicated than I previously thought.

I investigated the policy rationale for the war. I assessed the situations that led to the conflict. I learned that a political impasse, in all likelihood, culminated with the American withdrawal from Indochina. But the details were sketchy. I decided to explore the issues a bit further.

My goal was to examine the actions posed by those who concocted the Vietnam Conflict. But in order to accomplish that feat, I had to revisit the history of the war. [4] I came across several arguments, some of which suggested that domestic issues facilitated the end of the war.

My primary finds also suggested that domestic issues appeared to have had a dual impact on war efforts. On the one hand, a fervent desire to own aspects of the world led to the making of the war. In this case, a deeply rooted ideology provided the rationale for the American entry in Indochina. On the other hand, concerns at the domestic level seemed to have led to the taming of war efforts.

I was intrigued. I wanted to learn more about Vietnam. The problem is that I was able to examine the issues only as per the requirements set forth by the instructor. In the end, I wrote a final research paper, I got positive feedback from the instructor, and I completed the graduate program. I must say that the course did not satisfy my curiosity about the subject. I wanted to learn more about the conflict.

THE BOOK PROJECT

AFTER THE AFOREMENTIONED academic experience, I wanted to investigate the Vietnam War with more interest. For the class assignment, I approached the issues from a very broad perspective. Still, I did not really grasp the gist of the situation.

This is why I sought to compile a more coherent work about Vietnam. In order to complete the present work, I had to retrace my analytical steps from previous works. I reevaluated the issues. But I did so from a much narrower perspective.

I decided to turn the original class paper into a book. I revised my arguments. I refurbished some of the views I echoed in the paper. The present compilation is the result of these endeavors.

The more I learned about the war, the more it became obvious to me that the conflict was unsustainable. There were too many variables at play; there were too many actors involved in the conduct of the war itself. Managing war efforts was a challenge for most governmental officials.

It also seemed like concerns about the role America should play in world politics allowed Legislators to put the final nails in the coffin of the Vietnam War. Indeed, it could be said that the Legislature ended the American role in the war by withholding financial supports for the South Vietnamese military. Despite views to the contrary, one might say that the legislative branch did something that few people would have refuted back then.

It was conceivable that the Vietnam War would not last forever. The war was very unpopular. Most Americans wanted the conflict to end. The problem is that few commentators agreed with the manner in which Congress ended the war. Nonetheless, the legislative branch put an end to all speculations by ending the conflict on its own terms.

It must be said that this particular congressional act also provided a basis for many critics to blame Congress for the Vietnam debacle. But here, I proffer a different approach to the role Congress played in ending the war. That being said, this text is not a defense in favor of the United States Congress.

Although my initial finds were very interesting, they were not conclusive. I became very fascinated with the conflict. I wanted to learn more about the conduct of the war. I sought to investigate the topic further.

I must say; this book differs greatly from the school project referenced earlier. The present manuscript went through a rigorous editing process. Let me also point out that this work is not a revisionist account of the Vietnam War. This is to say that I will not assess the history of the war in depth here. With that confession out of the way, let me further point out that this opus offers a succinct, but thorough, examination of the Vietnam War, notably from a policy standpoint.

To Boss Ferrell

Acknowledgments

I WANT TO TAKE this opportunity to acknowledge several individuals for their unconditional contribution to my education. I want to thank them for their relentless support to my emotional and intellectual wellbeing. They include family members, friends, former teachers, and mentors.

I had the privilege of learning from their expertise in various fields during my elementary and secondary schooling (from 1978 to 1994). These people were part of my day (school day). They were part of my evenings (homework). Some of them were part of my personal growth in every aspect (my mother).

Each of these individuals, certainly, in his or her own way, inculcated a sense of inquisition in me. I am forever grateful for their support. I first learned about a place called Vietnam from these fine educators. I want to acknowledge these people in the present work because they laid down the foundation of my education.

I refer to these individuals as the pillars of my academic endeavors. They include, but are not limited to, the following:

My Mother (Mama)
Maître Cassion
Maître Gerald
Maître Jean-Charles (École Primaire/Primary School)
Maître Germain
Maître Casséus

Maître Michel
Mademoiselle Timothée
Maître Sanon
Maître Jean-Louis
Maître Baudelaire
Maître Roudler
Maître Chérie
Maître Alain
Maître Jean-Charles (École Secondaire/Secondary School)
Maître Edwidge
Maître Auguste
Maître Ludovic (Dodo)
Maître Pierre Paul Charles
Maître Fièvre
Among others…

INTRODUCTION

THE VIETNAM WAR was an unfortunate moment in human history. It was, for a fact, a horrific event in Indochina. It was also a tragic event in the history of modern warfare. This war was an unnecessary military venture, which led to an innumerable lost of lives.

No matter how you frame the debate, the conflict was a waste. It was also a *"Gaspillage"* of countless resources, which could have put Vietnam, not to mention several other nations in the Asian Continent, in a better economic shape. My position about the war is unequivocal. The Vietnam Conflict was a mistake; it was an irrefutable policy blunder.

The Americans could not contain the mess they made in Vietnam. Those who concocted, financed, and even conducted this misadventure, including civilian and military leaders, could not explain their failure in Indochina. After several years of hand-to-hand combats on the ground and after a number of diplomatic vicissitudes (including moments of triumphs), the Americans climatically ran away from the region without even acknowledging their failure to capture Vietnam.

To this day, the debate is still brewing regarding the degree to which America caused an enormous hardship in Indochina, mainly to the Vietnamese people. Discussions are still ongoing regarding the nature of the Vietnamese resistance as well. All the same, there is no consensus as to who could be considered the *bad guy* during the Vietnam madness.

Although the war took place several decades ago, most of the military clashes have been archived. To that degree, the history of the conflict is not a mystery; at least this is not the case for most observers. Yet, few people agree as to what truly took place in the jungles of Cambodia, Laos, and Vietnam between the 1960s and all the way to the mid-1970s. There is even less certitude as to what took place in Washington during the final months, weeks, days, and even hours of the conflict. But somehow, there is always a need to mince words about the Vietnam War.

Because there are so many viewpoints as to what transpired in Vietnam, it could be difficult to explain the conflict without being challenged or otherwise refuted. It might be appropriate to echo a popular cliché in this instance. On the basis thereof, it would not be farfetched to say that from most people's vantage point, "What happened in Vietnam must stay in Vietnam."

I wanted to unraveled one specific aspect about the war, which is often the subject of contentions. I wanted to explore the policy ramifications of the conflict. But I reckon that my views might not be in the majority. In any event, I hope to proffer a position about Vietnam, which is seldom echoed in the literature.

I did not want to examine the war based solely on my perception of what occurred in Indochina. I wanted to espouse a scientific approach to the conflict. But in order to reach my goals, I needed a sound theoretical framework. The problem is that locating a sensible theoretical tool was not that easy. It was certainly a daunting task in this instance.

SEARCHING FOR A FRAMEWORK

Vietnam was a complex military undertaken. Over the years, many inquirers have explored the conflict from various angles. Here, I wanted to approach Vietnam differently; I wanted to examine the ramifications of this military clash.

I sought to examine the events that transpired in both Indochina and Washington. The goal was to get a sense of the reason the war was fought. I also sought to familiarize myself with the actors who managed the conflict. But because of the intricate nature of the conduct of the war itself, I could not find firsthand accounts by policymakers.

After months of research, I could not come up with a theoretical framework, which would allow me to assess the policy rationale for the war. Since this work was originally a class assignment, the instructor recommended the use of three models, which had been proposed by Graham T. Allison.[1] I used the models as an intellectual tool, which allowed me to cater a better grasp of the issues.

The models were extremely useful; they allowed me concoct a coherent research paper about the war. I decided to utilize them in the present work as well. Here, the models serve as the foundation of my analysis.

The models had several limitations. For instance, I could not use them to explain every policy decision during the conflict. They provided little or no insights about the reality on the ground. They helped shed little or no light on the political struggles, which had been festering at home. The models could not help explain the limitations of branches of government, including the Legislature.

Although these models were helpful, the only way I could cater a bird's eye view of the Vietnam War was to examine its history in depth. But bear in mind that this text is not a rendition of the history of the war.

Moreover, the models could not help decipher the nature of the war. Vietnam was more complicated than pointing out that a mere political decision ended this military escapade. But the models had some important benefits. To that extent, they constitute the backbone of this manuscript.

The final portion of the book includes Chapters 13 through 16. This section is based on the application of the models to the Vietnam War. These chapters proffer an analysis of the withdrawal decision. But the analysis outlined here is limited to the degree to which the models could help make sense of the war, notably the decision to get out of Vietnam.

Allison originally developed the models in the 1970s. He did so as a means to elucidate the *Cuban Missile Crisis* of 1962 (*See* Chapters 7, 12, and 15 to learn more about the models). To that degree, my approach here is based on a narrow perspective about the Vietnam Conflict.

The nature of the Vietnam War could be hard to pin down. But I wanted to explore the political ramifications of the war. I examined the effects of the conflict both during and after combats officially ended. I ascertained the role of the individuals (i.e., the policymakers), the entities, and the atmosphere that instigated the conflict from a broader perspective.

I explored the possible reason(s) American officials felt that it was necessary to leave Vietnam in the manner that they did. But I only used Allison's models as a way to explain the policy rationale for the war. And so, I examined the actions and/or the omissions at the governmental level, which led to the end of the war.

In order to depict a larger tableau of what transpired in Vietnam, I consulted several outside sources as well. I explored both academic and governmental databases. I strolled through the web. I accessed governmental archives; I reviewed popular online libraries. I examined the views echoed in a number of blogs and websites.[2]

This work is not an exhaustive piece of literature. But that fact alone should not undermine its empirical value. The manuscript is the result of a research endeavor. It is well crafted to present a coherent argument about the Vietnam morass.

BOOK STRUCTURE

This book proffers a policy investigation of the Vietnam War. As such, it only explores the policy rationale that led to the decision to evacuate American embassy personnel from Saigon. At the time, this city was among the last American strongholds in Indochina.[3] But this work does not cater an in-depth examination of the war.

The document is divided in sixteen chapters. They are very short. The chapters are subdivided into five sections. They include: (a) The Vietnam Culprit (Chapters 1 to 2); (b) A war of pride (Chapters 3 to 5); (c) A tough war (Chapters 6 to 8); (d) The politics of war (Chapters 9 to 12); and (e) The withdrawal decision (Chapters 13 to 16).

The first few chapters provide an overview of the war, including its cost and the number of casualties. The middle segment of the text examines the political ramifications of the conflict. I will mostly explore the American side during the war.

Subsequent chapters re-assess the literature and summarize the chosen models. There, I examine the making of the withdrawal policy itself. The book culminates with a conclusion [final words] section, which summarizes the salient arguments echoed in the document.

The final segment reiterates the purpose of the book. It also assesses the limitations of the arguments purported therein. Without further delay, let us introduce the Vietnam War. Let us examine, albeit briefly, the worldview that instigated this military venture.

THE VIETNAM CULPRIT

BLAMING CONGRESS

CHAPTER ONE

1. A TREACHEROUS WAR

THE VIETNAM WAR had been ongoing for several decades when it abruptly ended in the mid-1970s. A few months prior, American officials appeared adamant in their desire to rid the region of Communism. But they evacuated Indochina and ran from Vietnam before a winner could be declared. Mainly for this reason, it is important to explore the cause (or the possible causes) that instigated this sudden policy reversal.

The year 1975 was decisive for a victory in the Vietnam Conflict. But it must also be noted that between 1969 and 1973, the United States had slowly, but steadily, reduced its military presence in the region. During that time, the number of military personnel [on Vietnamese territory of course] diminished considerably.

During the aforementioned period, American military presence in Indochina went from approximately 543,000 to only 50 active members, mostly throughout the Vietnamese region itself.[1] Proceeding on this track, it was conceivable that North Vietnamese forces would take control of the entire region as soon as they could galvanize the military capabilities to do so, which they eventually did in the spring of 1975.[2]

The pervading belief is that the Americans ran out of money. Washington could no longer sustain the South Vietnamese regime. I admit it; this argument has its merits. But I would not rely solely on this understanding in order to make my case either for or against the war.

Congress had rejected a request for military funding to South Vietnam. To that extent, it could be said that there was a money problem towards the end of the conflict. But I would also say that there is more to the issues than a mere funding disagreement.

The next logical question is why Congress refused to approve the military funding at this critical juncture. Answers are muddled. But most observers have come up with various explanations, theories, speculations, and hunches as to what happened in Washington. The problem is that many inquirers have approached the topic from a narrow perspective.

Some inquirers have approached the war from a military angle. Other observers have approached the conflict from a political lens. A few inquirers have also sought to ascertain the reason American Legislators refused to shore up the executive branch in its quest to provide aids to the South Vietnamese regime.

Nonetheless, the nature of the Vietnam War still eludes most observers. There is still a great mystery regarding the war. The perplexity is even greater when it comes to the last decision, which, hereafter, ended the war. Regrettably, this short volume alone could not elucidate that enigma. But even then, I will attempt, without fail I might say, to examine the nature of that conundrum.

In this short opus, I will not seek to impart blames. I will not even refute the contention that Congress played an important role in ending the war. The issue I will investigate in this text is whether Congress deserves all the blame for putting an end to this military adventure.

My investigation will center on one fundamental question. Should we blame Congress alone for the Vietnam debacle? In spite of the fact that Congress played an irrefutable role in both the making and the capitulation of the war, I would definitely answer the above question in the negative.

There is no way we could exclude American Legislators from the withdrawal decision or the decision-making process itself. But my position is that we must take into account the role of the other players. While I am inclined to support the idea that Congress played an eminent role in the withdrawal decision itself, I am also of the opinion that it may be vital to examine the actions and/or omissions of other actors. Based on that frame of mind, I will examine the war from several lenses.

In short, the issue at interests here is concerned with the reason the Americans withdrew from Vietnam. I understand that answers are not readily available. But we could speculate. Based on what is known about the war, we could concoct a number of probable reasons for its ill-timed end.

THE REASONS THE WAR ENDED

A plausible explanation for the withdrawal worth pointing out is that there was a growing fear, at the domestic level of course, that the United States' continued involvement in Indochina would lead to increased fighting, which would in due time lead to unnecessary casualties, more specifically among American soldiers and innocent civilians. There was a sense that the war had lasted too long and it was time to put an end to it. It could also be said that by that time, most members of Congress were under a lot of political pressure to end the war.

By the year 1973, the Vietnam War had become a toxic political hodgepodge. Selling the war was a difficult proposition. Even President Gerald Ford was not able to convinced prominent members of the Legislature that it was in the American government's interest to continue supporting the South Vietnamese regime. Although the President appealed to the legislative branch, in good faith some might say, the week following a resounding address to Congress, the Senate Armed Services Committee rejected a request logged by the executive branch for additional military assistance.[3] At that point, President Ford was scrambling to find allies in Congress that would be willing to truss the request.

On April 21, 1975, there was a bit of positive news in the White House. The House of Appropriations Committee approved a reduced amount for Vietnam. But the next day, the House Armed Services Committee refused to approve the new funds, which subsequently put a dent in the administration's attempt to secure the full approval.[4] At this particular juncture, any hope of reversing the political tide against the war was dead.

Another plausible reason was that, in Washington, the climate was not conducive for any political compromise. Oppositions to the war had been gaining tractions at an irreversible pace. As anticipated, the funding request was met with staunch opposition in both political aisles.[5] But this was not necessarily the only factual reason, which led Congress to reject the request.

There were other issues or other entities, which played a significant role in the final hours of the conflict. These actors also played a prominent role in the withdrawal decision. For instance, the President, as the head of the

American Government, played a significant role in galvanizing endorsement for war efforts. To say the least, President Ford's actions and/or inactions could also be understood as the roots of the withdrawal decision.

Other cabinet members played a role in creating the conditions for the conduct of the war. It could be said that these people were not, from within, on the same page with the legislative branch. They did not perforce share the President's ultimate concerns either. President Gerald Ford's legacy was on the line. But most cabinet members were undoubtedly impervious to this reality.

It might also be of a necessity to echo that the American public played a substantive role in shaping the debate in Washington. Because of all these reasons, it is paramount to evaluate the role of these actors in tandem. This is precisely what I propose in the present manuscript.

EXAMINING THE WITHDRAWAL DECISION

A political stalemate was not the only conceivable motive, which could explicate the cause or the possible reasons the war ended the manner that it did. Both chambers of Congress, which include the Senate and the House, had been structured to withstand political pressure. In order to find out what happened in Washington, we ought to look elsewhere.

From an institutional standpoint, the legislative setting could be considered as the perfect place for politics to thrive. Taking that fact on board, one might say that a political shock, on its own, could not have been the sole reason that ended the conflict. There ought to be other issues, which might have evaded the intellectual vigilance of a number of inquirers.

A lack of understanding about these issues could be the reason Vietnam is still a contentious topic. So many issues complicated war efforts. All the same, so many actors played a role in fermenting the conflict. Thus, it is important to examine the ramifications of war-making policies. It is essential that we explore the policy mechanism itself. This is where Allison's models could play an important role in helping us understand the nature of the policy, which led to the withdrawal of American troops from Vietnam.

The common belief is that the conduct of the war was a resounding fiasco. But that view also provided a rationale for oppositions to the war to gain steam. In consummation, such a reality also led to the demise of American politicians on both sides of the political aisle.

Let me propose this viewpoint. It is possible that most policy analysts have overlooked some key factors or some relevant aspects about the decision-making practices of the American government during the Vietnam ignominy. It must also be noted that the war changed American foreign politics. It did so in many ways. For example, because of Vietnam, most Americans do not trust their government, notably when it comes to engaging American troops in international conflicts.

From a policy standpoint, Vietnam is still a mystery. To this day, the extent of the issues that exacerbated the war has remained unascertained. This is precisely the essence of the discussions I would like to proffer in this paperback.

It could be adumbrated that most politicians [in Washington] were aware of the possible impacts of their refusal to back up war efforts. Thus, it seems reasonable to argue that a mere political opposition would not have been enough motives to stifle a larger policy framework, which had been guiding the American involvement in Southeast Asia for many years. Vietnam was the ultimate prize in Indochina. The Americans wanted to win that prize at all costs.

I would also echo that there was a larger force at play, which derailed America's interests in the region. Perhaps, that force was fueled by public oppositions to the war itself. At the time, public disdain for the war had a tremendous effect on the political discourse in Washington. But I also understand that it might be difficult to assess the extent of the war and possibly the reason for its end based primarily on hunches and speculations.

We must decipher the underlying factors that made it possible for Congress to refuse to fund the war. We need to ascertain the possible reason [or reasons] this conflict ended independently of what the American President wanted and what he actively sought. But I reckon that the issues are not that simple. Nonetheless, it is paramount to examine the possible ulterior motive(s) Congress might have had for refusing to approve the funding request in the end. In that sense, we must examine the issues within in a larger parameter.

A CHAOTIC EVACUATION

An important metric I will use in order to examine the withdrawal decision centers on the chaotic evacuation from Saigon. The American Embassy there was an important or perhaps a strategic reference point for the United States. The month of April was relatively a very active period. Since the beginning of the month until its remaining days, even hours, the American military had been working laboriously to evacuate Embassy personnel throughout the region.

During the wee hours of the withdrawal day, the decisions had already been made—orders had been given—to the appropriate chain of command (of course) for execution. Most governmental agencies, notably the concerned branches of government, including the military, were already in the implementing phase of those decisions. There was a sense of an impending doom or an imminent threat onto the American military and civilian personnel in certain parts of Vietnam.

The most remarkable evacuation occurred in Saigon, the capital of Vietnam at the time. There, Marine Helicopters could be seen landing frantically on rooftops. At that point, it was unambiguous that the U.S. military was scrambling to find a safe avenue in order to rescue stranded Embassy personnel and local Vietnamese residents. Many of these individuals were desperate to flee the looming fall of the city.

As it had been awaited, immediately after the evacuation, the city fell under the control of North Vietnamese fighters. This iconic moment is commonly referred to as *"The Fall of Saigon."*[6] It was also part of the initial acts towards the end of a long and treacherous military venture in Indochina. Examining the *Saigon flight* is the quintessence of this work.

SAVING SOUTH VIETNAM

On the surface, the Ford administration appeared to have done all that it could in order to avert a defeat in Vietnam. The President, including several members of his cabinet, endeavored relentlessly to avoid a political defeat at home. For a short period, the battleground (i.e., the political battleground itself) was no longer in Vietnam. Rather, it was in Washington.

In the end, the war ended despite the desires of the President of the United States. The conflict culminated just like a fish tail (or *finir en queue de poisson*). The Americans withdrew from Vietnam in spite of the executive branch's efforts for a different outcome. To this day, questions are legions as to why a withdrawal decision was the best outcome of the Vietnam War.

What happened in Vietnam? What led to this stunning trounce in American foreign Policy? Beyond any doubt, the Saigon evacuation was not the result many observers (both in Washington and in other parts of the country) had anticipated, though a number of them wanted the war to end.

I could say with confidence that President Gerald Ford did not seek such a conclusion. Just a few months before the final decision, the executive branch, which was headed by President Ford himself, seemed very keen on preserving the sanctity of South Vietnam. But there is no doubt that President Ford's efforts did not yield positive results. Still, we must ascertain what went wrong in Washington.

Other questions might include the following: What stifled the executive branch in the end? Who is the culprit? Who deserves the blame? Of course, some commentators might say that the ford Administration played its role to the letter and until the last minute. From this angle, the understanding is that Congress was the sole obstacle, which the President could not surmount on his own.

President Gerald Ford had a clear message. From his vantage point, it was of an utmost necessity to save South Vietnam. But it seemed like no one in Congress was willing to listen to the President of the United States on the matter of Vietnam either way. Understandably, Congress became the default culprit. Let us ascertain whether this view is justified or not.

I am not convinced that Congress, on its own, derailed efforts to win the war. Those that suggest the opposite viewpoint are manifestly intransigent in their assessment of the situation. As insinuated earlier, there were other players involved. Thus, it is important to examine how these players influenced the legislative branch in the end.

I am inclined to believe that when a victory was no longer possible, Congress felt an obligation to act. As per its role within the federal government, Congress had the power to end the American involvement in the conflict. But I would not categorize that act, in and of itself, as a deliberate attempt on the part of the Legislators to end the war unilaterally.

I reckon that Congress was part of the decision makers that endeavored to end the conflict. But the extent of the role the Legislature played in the last moments of the war is not clear. My point is that we may never be sure about what truly took place in Washington. That being said, we could speculate, in truth of course, as to what plausibly happened.

With that said, let me also note that I do not want to hypothesize willy-nilly about the role each actor played during the conduct of the war. Here, I propose a scientific approach in order to examine the final decision to end the war. From my vantage point, this is the best way to shed some lights on what most likely transpired in Washington in the spring of 1975.

We must ascertain, at least as surgically as possible, what led to the premature end of the Vietnam War. In this instance, we need to understand what prompted President Ford to come to the realization that he had no other alternative but to bring home all the remaining American personnel on Vietnamese territory. Why did the President capitulate? Why did he throw in the towel, so to speak? Clearly, it was not because of a lack of trying on the part of the President to save his legacy.

THE LAST MANEUVERS

The presumption is that the Ford administration worked arduously in order to prevent Congress from rejecting its request for South Vietnam. It was widely believed that the executive branch endeavored tenaciously in order to persuade influential members of the House of Representative [notably powerful committee members] that it would be in the nation's best interest to continue supporting the South Vietnamese regime. Evidently, not all these efforts paid off in the end.

On April 10, 1975, President Ford went to Congress and gave a passionate speech before the House of Representative about his intentions in Vietnam. The President reiterated the necessity for Congress to *"Enforce"* the American government's engagement to provide Vietnam with the economic and military aids that the country needed in order to sustain itself—which includes its military—in the conflict.[7]

Most observers viewed this move as a desperate attempt by the President to sway dissidents in his camps. They argued that President Ford knew [or must have known] that it would be an uphill battle to convince reluctant members of Congress to give their blessing to war efforts. By that time, it was common knowledge that the Vietnam War had polarized the country, both socially and politically. Under this political climate, it may be the case that this speech was President Ford's final maneuver to save his foreign policy legacy. Perhaps this was also a way for the President to salvage the war policy heritage of his predecessors, notably Richard Nixon.

The polarization, which patently resulted from the conduct of the war itself, was having an effect on the political spectrum. Local pressures to end the conflict were mounting. Members of Congress could no longer ignore their constituency on this matter. In other words, President Ford knew or perhaps should have known that Congress was in a tough spot politically.

The efforts projected by the Ford administration were indeed in futility. In the end, the President failed to convince dissident voices in Congress to vote in favor of the request. The legislators sequentially rejected the financial aid request for South Vietnam.

At the end of the day, President Ford was left with little or no other options. Just as a self-fulfilling prophecy, the American government found itself in the impossibility to provide financial assistance to South Vietnam, which in turn had a tremendous impact on war efforts. Does this mean that Congress should bear the responsibility of ending the Vietnam Conflict? Let us examine the issues a bit further.

CHAPTER TWO

2. MIXED VIEWS ABOUT CONGRESS

FROM THE HALLS OF HISTORY, Congress has often been identified as the sole culprit for the reason the Vietnam Conflict ended in disarray. But for anti-war activists, Congress did what was necessary to save the country. The American Legislature was considered the only legitimate force capable of deterring the executive branch from continuing to engage the country in this never-ending conflict. At long last, Congress did just that.

The argument often evoked by anti-war activists is that Congress exerted its constitutional prerogative to intervene in a war that was evidently damaging to the country's interests.[1] But is there any truth to that apprehension? Presently, there is not a common ground as to what really happened at the governmental level during the Vietnam War. Nonetheless, I would definitely answer the previous question in the affirmative.

I must emphasize that some observers might refute the previous assertion. They might point out that Congress did not always play a prominent role in foreign policy issues. Thus, the apparent Congressional intrusion during the Vietnam War was a peculiarity from the position the legislature often espoused in the country's foreign policy.

Historically speaking, foreign policy has always been in the purview of the executive branch. The reason for that reality is not obvious. Certainly, the legislative branch of the federal government has a constitutional authority to authorize wars. On the other hand, however, the Legislature had habitually relegated the authority to deploy troops abroad and the flexibility to manage war efforts to the executive branch. But somehow, Vietnam changed the role of the players in the foreign policy game; Congress changed it all.

Incontestably, the Vietnam War redefined American foreign policy matters. One might say that the conflict represents a breaking point in the dynamic between the legislative and the executive branches of government. Some might also say that Congress rather reclaimed its constitutional authority in matters pertaining to wars.

It is undeniable that during Vietnam, the American Legislature reasserted itself in foreign policy. But it did so rather preponderantly, one might even say. Still, that fact alone does not perforce explain the circumstance (or the realities) that led to this dramatic change the policy rituals of veteran politicians in Washington.

It is irrefutable that, for a number of years, foreign policy initiatives had been relegated to the jurisdiction of the executive branch. But towards the end of the Vietnam Conflict, Congress evidently flexed its muscles and reclaimed that authority. To that extent, there is a need to ascertain the reason [or reasons] members of the Legislature felt it was necessary to reassert Congress' foreign policy role in this particular issue.

The debate is still ongoing regarding the essence of the role Congress played in Vietnam. There are still questions concerning the true amount of power Congress genuinely holds in foreign policy initiatives. That is to say, when it comes to the role the Legislature played in determining the course of the Vietnam War, answers are still murky. At this point, I am not that much concerned with the conduct of the war itself. Rather, the focus of my analysis is on the actions and/or the omissions of the people who acted conjointly or else in order to end the Vietnam Conflict.

The question that is worthy of our attention here is what exactly incited Congress to reject the military aid request, knowing the potential drawbacks of such an act. Since answers are not clear, we could revert to the domestic pressure argument to make sense of what happened. But depending on whom you ask the above question, answers could vary considerably. My point is that, no matter how one approaches this issue, there might be an array of diverging viewpoints. Regrettably, I could not rebuff them all here.

The position commonly echoed in the literature is that Congress deserves the blame for the Vietnam mess. I disagree with that viewpoint. Let me explain why I do not subscribe to that understanding.

My view is that Congress alone could not end the Vietnam War. There were too much at stake for the other players to sit idly by and let a congressional decision derail a foreign policy initiative, which had been in effect in Indochina for a very long time. I must admit it; the challenge in this text is to offer enough evidence to corroborate that refutation as cogently as possible.

BLAMING CONGRESS

Most observers have denoted that the congressional refusal to fund South Vietnam was among the major events that forced the Americans to adopt a different policy direction in the war. The argument here is that the refusal to support South Vietnam forced the American government to end its commitments in Indochina. That is to say, Congress' actions unilaterally led to the premature end of the conflict.

There is a bit of illogic to point out in this instance. The United States was not at war in Indochina in 1975. As we will see later in the text, the war had officially ended two years (i.e., 1973) before the Ford administration entered into what appeared to be a wrestling match with the legislative branch. But other observers have contended that since the aid was necessary for the South Vietnamese regime to maintain its military endeavors, Congress is indeed responsible for South Vietnam's defeat.

Veritably, this argument could be difficult to refute. Despite that conjecture, however, it might become imperative to point out faulty logics in the many claims that are often echoed in the literature about the role the American Legislature played in winding down war efforts. As inferred earlier, Congress does not deserve all the blames in the Vietnam fiasco.

Other commentators have argued that it does not matter whether the Americans had been involved directly or otherwise in Vietnam; it was common knowledge in Washington that the South Vietnamese regime would not last long in the conflict without the financial backing of the United States. To that degree, depriving the Southern regime of the financial support that it greatly needed was akin to providing an edge to North Vietnamese fighters. From most observers' vantage point, Congress did just that.

I do not dispute the relevance of the refusal to provide financial assistance to South Vietnam. This act irrefutably played a role in the final decision to withdraw completely from the region. The availability of money or a sustainable funding source could be an excellent indicator for success in any military conflict. Considering that fact, I would concede that Congress deserves some blame. But I do not subscribe to the notion that the American legislature, on its own of course, deserves all the blame for Vietnam.

Vietnam was no ordinary conflict. This war lasted more than three decades. It is unconceivable that a derisory Congressional refusal to approve a military aid package would be the sole factor that led to the demise of this military venture. Other factors are worth taking into account as well. But for now, let us explore some of the motives that, to all appearances, led to the end of the war. Let us explore, albeit summarily, the cost of the Vietnam War.

THE COST OF THE VIETNAM WAR

Views broadly differ as to the reason(s) the American government was unable to secure a victory in Vietnam. For instance, observers hold opposing views as to who won the war in the end. It is also disputed whether North Vietnamese fighters were aided by foreign fighters, including fighters from China. But what is certain is the war was brutal.

The battles took a toll on both the American military and the people of Vietnam. The amount of human suffering was staggering. The amount of casualties sustained by the different parties involved in the conflict was also incommensurable. But the war was also costly from a financial standpoint. Let us examine that aspect of the war, albeit summarily here.

The financial cost of the war, specifically on the American side, was very disheartening. To this day, the true cost of this military venture is unsettled. But by way of estimation, it is believed that the Vietnam War cost approximately $173 billion, which, in 2003, was estimated around $770 billion.[2] Other estimations that are currently floating on the Internet list the amount of $1 trillion (in current monetary value).[3] This amount also includes the cost of paid out in benefits, which is totaled around $270 billion.[4]

Other estimates are more conservative. They typically list a lesser amount. For instance, in a report prepared for Congress by Stephen Daggett, the cost of the war was approximated (between the years 1965 and

1975) around $111 billion, which would amount [approximately] around $686 billion in today's monetary value.[5]

Regardless of the real amount of money that had been dispensed during the conflict, most people resented the fact that American officials spent a lot of money in order to maintain the course in Vietnam. Anti-war advocates often contend that it is precisely because of this financial burden, Congress was able to put an end to this complete waste of resources. Indeed, Congress utilized its power to control agency funding, also known as the *Power of the Purse,* in order to halt the United States military role in Indochina. Later in this volume, I will discuss the role of Congress more substantively.

SUMMARY OF ARGUMENTS

To recapitulate some of the points articulated here thus far, I am not at all convinced that Congress is the only entity that led to the demise of the American government in Vietnam. Other actors played a significant role in creating the condition for the war to end the manner that it did. Here, I want to put an emphasis on these actors.

In order to characterize some of the arguments I will proffer in subsequent chapters, let me point out that this book does not seek to minimize the effects of the war per se. It is not a repudiation of the actions or inactions taken by any of the parties involved. This work does not seek to misrepresent the events that took place both in Vietnam and in Washington.

What I am saying here is that the present work does not aim at mischaracterizing the role of the actors that participated in the decision to instigate the war. It does not seek to praise those who, after all, ended the conflict. All the same, I do not seek to portray any one side as more brutal than the other was.

Vietnam was a military conflict. Wars are never pretty. In this regard, I do not feel obligated to hold back my position against the war. But I do not wish to project a politically correct argument in this document either. What I am saying is that I do not feel bound to alter certain aspects of the conflict in an attempt to patronize one side to the detriment of another.

I will endeavor arduously to offer an objective assessment of the war. I will labor to convey my apprehension about Vietnam from the lens of those who witnessed it, either personally or vicariously. I will also include the views of those who did not exigently experience the conflict either near or far.

If you have read this text up until this point, you should have a good grasp of the gist of the issues I will debate hereinafter. But I must also applaud your determination and your interest in this work. From this point forward, I will outline the history of the Vietnam War.

Let me also warn you that some of the arguments I will purport within the next few chapters might appear repetitive. That being said, I will relate many of these issues from different angles. But the theme of the document itself centers on the notion that the end of the Vietnam War was not the doing of one entity. I will elaborate on what I mean by that.

A War Of Pride

Not America's War

CHAPTER THREE

3. A MILITARY GRAVEYARD

VIETNAM IS CONSIDERED the graveyard of the American military. Although this statement may sound too strong or too pompous, it is not the product of my own invention. This understanding captures the reality, which many American soldiers experienced during the conflict. This war drained many American warriors both physically and emotionally.

During the Vietnam War, a very high number of soldiers perished in Indochina. Those that survived this ordeal often carry the physical or the emotional scars to prove that they had been part of it. Vietnam could never be an easily forgotten chapter in American military's olden times.

This was certainly a very difficult moment for the United States as the military beacon of the world. There they were and they were being hammered on all sides by a bunch of jungle warriors. Many of these fighters did not receive any sophisticated training; they did not possess top-notch armaments or other types of military hardware. But why were these people able to set back the Americans? Unfortunately, that is not one of the goals of the present work.

What is clear is that the Americans were not up to the task of defeating North Vietnamese fighters. This reality was certainly not the outcome that many American observers had anticipated. This military hindrance was not projected from the Vietnamese peasants in any scenario. It is fair to say that the Americans did not foresee such a resistance from Vietnam when they set out to conquer Indochina.

The Vietnam War had innumerable repercussions on the country as a whole (i.e., the United States). It had an effect on various social aspects, including the country's political past. Say what you want; but this war is among "The most misguided political and military crusade in American history."[1]

In the Jungle of Laos, Cambodia, and Vietnam, the limits of the American Army were stretched thin.[2] This wonderful military machine was tested to a point where the effects of the war can still be apparent today. Most observers are convinced that Vietnam was more lethal for the American military than any other wars it fought before.

It is true; the war created an incommensurable amount of veterans. Many of these veterans are disabled and crippled.[3] But for some observers, Vietnam War veterans have been ignored.

The pervading understanding is that, just like the Vietnam War, many of the people who fought in the conflict have been snubbed and pushed aside.[4] Some of them *"Became bitter and angry."*[5] The common view in most military circles is that Vietnam veterans are *"Truly the lost Americans."*[6]

A GOOD WAR

It must be noted that other observers have also painted a more allegoric picture about Vietnam veterans. For instance, despite arguments to the contrary, the common presupposition is that most American fighters had a positive experience both during and after the conflict. The understanding is that the majority of Vietnam veterans were satisfied with their participation in the war itself.

The belief is that the Vietnam War was not a malaise for most military personnel. For instance, it is believed that approximately 91% of Vietnam War veterans are glad to have served in the war.[7] It is further estimated that 74% of these veterans confided that they would take part in the conflict again despite knowing the outcome.[8]

When it comes to transitioning into society, the understanding is that 85% of Vietnam veterans have made successful transitions to civilian life.[9] They also have the lowest unemployment rate than the same non-vet age groups.[10] Their personal income exceeds that of non-veterans of the same age group by more than 18%.[11]

For the same reason, it is also believed that a whopping 87% of Americans hold Vietnam War veterans to high esteem.[12] The argument here is that, regardless of the nature of the war, most people think highly of Vietnam War veterans. I am sure that for some observers, this number might be hard to believe. This figure is shocking, considering the degree of the tantrum most Americans acted out during the war.

Based on the previous assessments, could we say that the Vietnam War was worth it? The answer would be irrefutably in the negative. The conflict was a mistake in American military history. From the perspective of an array of historians, the United States military failed miserably in Vietnam. American commanders had no excuse, other than their lack of training and skills to defeat the cunning North Vietnamese guerrilla warriors (many of them are still alive today).

Based on the above logic, some observers are of the opinion that Vietnam was a lost cause since the start. American fighters did not know who, what, why, or where they were fighting. But most Vietnamese fighters had a unique perspective as to whom they were fighting, the reason they were fighting, and where they were fighting. They were motivated to win, while American soldiers were outwardly motivated to fight.

THE REAL WAR

Initially, many Americans had no personal qualms in Vietnam. But this was only true until the moment they started to witness the carnage, which had been brought in their ranks by North Vietnamese fighters. At some point during the war, notably on the American side, it seemed like the fighting was all about avenging the lives of fallen comrades. This sentiment led to an array of human rights violations, other abuses, and unconscionable atrocities. But it would not be whimsical to say that this regrettable aspect of the war had been deliberately undermined by American officials.

There were many instances of staggering human suffering during the Vietnam War. As Nick Turse pointed out in his book *"Kill Anything That Moves: The Real American war in Vietnam"* (2013), there was a well-orchestrated propaganda machine, on the American side of course, to cover up some of the most atrocious aspects of the war. This was done specifically to hide events that involved American military personnel in Vietnam.

To be clear, I do not lump all military personnel in the same basket. Here, I am referring to military staff that went rogue. I am also referring to other types of misconducts, which American troops perpetrated in retaliation to aggressions that they witnessed and/or experienced in the region.

The Vietnam Conflict was very tragic. Victims did not only come from the ranks of the enemy. The majority of the people who were victimized were not on the battlefield per se. Many of the casualties were not perforce related to military fighting [or combat related]. The civilian population was often targeted and abused by both Vietnamese fighters and American soldiers (*See* Chapter 6). But this side of the conflict is seldom depicted accurately, as Turse noted in his book.[13]

The American government seldom acknowledged its fair share in the many atrocities that took place in Vietnam. There was an intentional cover-up of some of the most atrocious conducts of American military personnel. Let us further explore the nature of that conspiracy.

THE COVER-UP

There had been a deliberate attempt to portray the Vietnam War in the most positive light as possible, at least from an American perspective. Incidents that did catch public attention were usually recounted as isolated issues, which only reflected the acts of rogue soldiers. Stories about the many war crimes and the extent of the civilian suffering that transpired during battles are regularly discussed within the context of a single incident.[14] But those who witnessed the military clashes had a very different perspective as to what truly transpired in Vietnam.

American soldiers were fighting a different war from the one the enemy had been engaged in the jungle of Laos, Vietnam, and Cambodia. As likely as not, the Americans were not fundamentally defending a core belief in the region. A popular belief in most literary corners is that American leaders sought to prevent the expansion of Communism in the Southeast corridor. For the most part, they endeavored arduously (in futility of course) in order to accomplish that goal.

The Vietnamese people, on the other hand, wanted freedom from foreign dominion, including from both the French and the Americans. But unlike American fighters, the enemy had all the incentives to withstand the negative effects of the war. They were fighting for their survival.

Initially, it was unthinkable that the *"Viet Minh"* fighters could even resist the wrath of the United States' military might, including its infantry, naval power, and air force. The reality is that Vietnam was not a conventional type of warfare. The war was brutal; casualties were equally horrific on all the sides involved in the conflict. To that extent, having a superior military power appeared inconsequential in Vietnam.

Overall, it could be said that Vietnam was not an ordinary military event. The war helped redefined several notions pertaining to military prowess, including the idea that advanced technologies could be translated into superior military advantages. What seemed to matter the most during Vietnam was the desire of the enemy to fight until the end. Many Vietnamese fighters unequivocally displayed such a desire; they did so incessantly.

Where is Vietnam Located? What led to the war? In other words, who initiated the conflict? We must also ascertain how the United States got involved in this military venture. The following pages will recount the history of the war. I will also attempt to answer the above questions as cogently as possible.

Before we tackle the essence of this military clash, let us familiarize ourselves with Vietnam (as a country of course). Let us explore Vietnam in terms of its geography and population. Let us examine the genesis of the war at the most intrinsic level.

VIETNAM: GEOGRAPHY AND POPULATION

Where is Vietnam located? Vietnam is located in the Asian continent, more precisely in Southeast Asia.[15] The country is adjacent to China, Lao People's Democratic Republic (or PDR), and Cambodia. The country shares a border with China in the North. In the West, Vietnam is bordered by Lao PDR and Cambodia. In the East, the country borders with the South China Sea.

Presently, the capital of Vietnam is Hanoi. The former capital and largest city in Vietnam used to be Ho Chi Minh City. This city was also known as Saigon.[16] The current population of the Vietnamese landscape is estimated at 90,630,000 (as of 2014). Vietnam is considered the 13th most populated country in the world.[17] The country has a population density of 295 people per square kilometer.[18]

The country's area is calculated around 332,698 square kilometers of land and approximately 21,140 square kilometers of water. From a geographic standpoint, Vietnam is considered the 66th largest nation in the world.[19] At sea, the country is enjoined by Indonesia, Malaysia, Philippines, and Thailand.

THE GENESIS OF THE VIETNAM WAR

How the Vietnam War started? There are many accounts as to when or how the conflict itself started. But when I speak of Vietnam, it must be clear that I am referring to the war between the United States and the Viet Cong Forces. It is also important to point out that military skirmishes had already begun when the Americans got involved in the conflict.

The common belief is that this was a revolutionary war between France and Vietnamese peasants. Over the years, however, the war evolved into a geopolitical struggle for control and self-determination. But this was mostly the case on the American side. Vietnamese fighters had other motives in the fight. As insinuated earlier, Vietnam was also a fight for survival, at least for most North Vietnamese fighters.

In the 1800s, France colonized Vietnam and began taking control of the country's natural resources. At the time, Vietnam was known for its rice fields and thriving rubber productions. France also took over Laos and Cambodia. The three colonized countries became known as the French Indochina.

Because of the colonization, French colonialists amassed a considerable amount of riches. In a short period, the peasants lost their land and they became subjugated to a new ruling class, the wealthy French colonialists. In July 1954, France was driven out of Vietnam after one hundred years of colonial rule.[20] Between 1954 and 1975, Vietnam was America's war.

In the beginning, Vietnam was not in the forefront of American scrutiny. From a domestic standpoint, Vietnam was not of any interest. Few Americans knew about Vietnam. An even fewer number of citizens understood the reason their government was involved in the region.

Overtime, this tableau drastically changed. Little by little, domestic interests in Vietnam grew considerably. The problem is that the more

Americans learned about Vietnam and the more they got a sense of what was truly occurring in Indochina, few people supported the American government's actions in the region. Still, there were those who supported the war no matter what. As a result, the war led to a rift in American society.

On the other hand, there were those who opposed the war since the beginning. These people were relentless. Consistently, they hardened their posture. They got even more radical in their views towards the end of the conflict. They sought the end of hostilities at any rate.

For the most part, these people wanted America to withdraw from Vietnam at all costs. Those who supported the conflict took a firm position on the matter. But some of them acknowledged that there was a need for a different direction. The war polarized the country in many ways.

At this point, an important conjecture to point out is that the foundation of the war was very shaky. American officials did not seem to have a clear motive for engaging in military battles in Indochina. When the negative effects of the war started to hit home, anti-war sentiments grew rapidly. In many cases, anti-war reactions were visceral and, at times, violent. But what was the reason [or possible reasons] the Americans got involved in the Vietnam War in the first place? Let us explore further.

ENTERING THE CONFLICT

If we were to examine the Vietnam Conflict based on the precise moment America entered the region, we might say that the war officially began around 1945. This was the mostly acknowledged moment that President Harry Truman offered aids to the French. In the beginning, the United States' contribution and ultimate support were monetary.

Gradually, however, the Americans provided other types of supports to the French, including military expertise and equipments. Despite the American's generous financial aids and military assistance, the French had been defeated pitifully in North Vietnam. But in theory, the United States was not at war in the region until North Vietnamese fighters [presumably] attacked a United States Naval ship, which had been patrolling the Gulf of Tonkin. Later, I will discuss the Tonkin attack in more detail.

The Vietnam War officially started when Congress passed a resolution, authorizing President Lyndon Baines Johnson the power to go to war with

North Vietnam. A fair portrayal of the American involvement in Vietnam suggests that this was not a haphazard war or a fortunate military venture. From a practical standpoint, the United States had been involved in the region militarily long before the Tonkin incident. The American government supported France unconditionally.

The French did not enter the conflict for the same reason the Americans did. The French involvement was a reaction to a local uprising, whereas, the American involvement was, on the face of it all, ideologically driven. Like as not, the Americans sought to establish a Hegemonic dominion throughout Southeast Asia.

What I am saying is that the American entry in Indochina was not by fortune. This act was very much on par with the Truman Doctrine.[21] In short, it could be said that the United States did not get involved in the Vietnam morass by accident. Rather, it was a strategically guided decision. That decision was unquestionably based on a larger policy framework.

Unquestionably, there were greater motives for the American involvement in the conflict. But the understanding is that the Americans wanted to maintain economic access in the region, deterring the rise of a regional Hegemon, discouraging conflict and maintaining regional stability, and promoting human rights and democracy.[22] Regardless of the rationale for entering into the conflict, Vietnam was not necessarily America's problem; at least this was not the case initially.

As mentioned earlier, the French were entangled in an existential fight with a group of rebels known as the Viet Minh.[23] At that point, the Americans were not part of the conflict itself. But they did sponsor the French in many aspects.

When the French were defeated, the Americans took over the region. They subsequently inherited the many military skirmishes that ensued. Therewithal, the Vietnam Conflict could be understood as two separate wars: a war that was fought by the French and the other by the Americans. At this point in the document, it is important to examine these conflicts independently.

CHAPTER FOUR

4. THE FIRST VIETNAM WAR

IN 1945, VIETNAM declared its independence from France. Nonetheless, both France and the United States ignored the call for the independence. Instead, French authorities sought to ramp up their control of the region and proceeded to crush Vietnamese dissidents.

For a while, it seemed as though the French were going to prevail. However, the development of World War II brought a big change in Indochina. That change had a substantial effect in the conduct of the military skirmishes between the French and Vietnamese fighters.

A Communist leader by the name of Ho Chi Minh launched an army, also known as the *"Viet Minh Army."* He sought to wage a war against the French colonialists. Ho Chi Minh and his men orchestrated a rebellion against the French military, which had been established in the region since 1888.

In 1946, a revolutionary war started between the Viet Minh Army and the French Army. Ho Chi Minh's goal was to liberate Vietnam from French rule. At the time, this was considered an ambitious objective. On all counts, Ho Chi Minh would achieve this goal, despite many expectations to the contrary.

In what could only be dubbed as a move to protect the *"Imperialist Brotherhood,"* which was *de rigueur* at the time, President Harry Truman decided to lend America's unconditional assistance to the French. At that point, the United States offered its unyielding support to French authorities.

France, on the other hand, was locked in a fight with several Vietnamese peasants to continue its grip over the country.

It is worth reiterating that, during the aforementioned epoch, America was only acting as a surrogate military force in Southeast Asia. Although the real reason America got involved in the war is somewhat unclear, it is widely believed that President Truman wanted to prevent Ho Chi Minh from taking over Indochina. Many observers are of the opinion that the United States sought to prevent the so-called *"Domino Effect"* throughout the region.

Little by little, the Americans sought to establish their dominion over Vietnam. But this endeavor became a part of a larger foreign policy in Southeast Asia. It was, on the face of it, a strategic means to prevent Communism from taking hold in Indochina. Thus, the American involvement in the region was initially a geopolitical move.

The arguments offered by most political analysts at the time centered on the notion that, a Communist Vietnam would have some serious repercussion throughout the region. Such a scenario could potentially change the geopolitical landscape, ardent supporters of the American involvement in Vietnam echoed.

During that period, another viewpoint was gaining prominence in various intellectual circles. The argument often articulated by most observers centered on the notion that a Communist expansion throughout Southeast Asia must be prevented at all costs.[1] At the time, Vietnam was at the center of that foreign policy discourse. The Vietnam War was clearly the result of this worldview.

The "SEATO" Accord

In the summer of 1954, France was losing its grip over Indochina. After several battles, it became evident that Vietnamese Nationalist forces, under the command of General Vo Nguyen Giap, had inflicted serious setbacks to the French military.[2] As a result, the French agreed to a peaceful accord. In Geneva, Switzerland, both parties signed the pact commonly known as *"The Geneva Peace Accords."*

At the time, the United States government did not back up the accord. Then Secretary of State, John Foster Dulles, sought a different alternative to the Geneva agreement. Many voices within the American government echoed that the accord afforded too much power to the Communist Party of Vietnam.[3]

The Geneva Accords allowed South and North Vietnam to exist, albeit temporarily, as separate nations.[4] Of course, this outcome did not sit well with the Americans. Subsequently, the American government worked arduously in order to undermine the Geneva agreements.

The Americans proposed a new agreement, known as the Southeast Asia Treaty Organization (also known as the SEATO), which would help rebuild the nation.[5] This organization was established in 1954 by countries like the United States, the United Kingdom, Australia, New Zealand, France, Pakistan, the Philippines, and Thailand.[6] The official objective of that organization was a direct response to the perceived threat posed by the rise of Communism throughout the Southeast Asian corridor.[7]

The creation of this organization had a parallel purpose. Using the SEATO as a scapegoat, Dwight D. Eisenhower, the American President at the time, helped created the Government of the Republic of Vietnam (also known as GVN or South Vietnam). The South Vietnamese regime was supposed to serve as a geopolitical portal for the United States and its allies in the region.

The United States poured an incalculable amount of military, political, and economic aid in the creation of the South Vietnamese regime.[8] Effectively, the Americans had taken over France's place as an *imperial* force in the region. Of course, they also inherited the resentment that many Vietnamese dissidents felt for France.

THE TWO VIETNAMESE STATES

In 1954, Vietnam was divided in two separate countries. The French remained in control of the South, while the Viet Minh Army took over the North. The country became known as two separate entities: North Vietnam (or Communist Vietnam) and South Vietnam (or Anti-Communist Vietnam).

When the country was divided into two independent nations, the United States maintained (if not increased) its role in the region. The belief at the time is that the American government's primary goal was to undermine the Communist regime in the north. Meanwhile, the United States continued to lend its support to the Southern Vietnamese regime.

But it must also be noted that since the late 1950s, South Vietnam had been engaged in constant military scuffles with its Northern (Communist) neighbor.

While the Americans offered more support to the regime in the South, they got involved deeper in the conflict itself. The American government became entrenched in the outcomes of the war.[9] As opposed to being a military asset and a political ally of the South Vietnamese regime, gradually, the United States became a party in the conflict. The Americans got irreversibly embroiled in the region.

Soon, there was a Communist uprising in the South. By that point, France had slowly diminished its role in the region. The United States, on the other hand, as the guarantor of the French ideal in Indochina, continued its support of the regime in the South.

The Tonkin incident provided another reason for the Americans to get deeply involved in the region.[10] President Lyndon Johnson obtained authorization from Congress to take military actions in Vietnam.[11] That moment marked the beginning of a new era in the war. To learn more, see chapter nine (A Broad Mandate).

The congressional authorization to engage the enemy on the battlefield changed the course of the war. It also influenced the extent of the American involvement in the region. It was the start of a new war. It was the beginning of the second war. Let us explore the nature of that conflict further.

CHAPTER FIVE

5. THE SECOND VIETNAM WAR

IN 1964, THE UNITED STATES role in the Vietnam Conflict changed drastically. Because of the Gulf of Tonkin incident, the American government had a legitimate reason to fight directly against the Northern regime.[1] The belief is that the Americans were dragged into the war because of the Tonkin attack. But some observers have questioned the veracity of that understanding.

Even after the Tonkin incident, the Americans had not really committed their full military power to the war. But since Congress authorized military actions against North Vietnam, the American military build-up in Indochina increased considerably. By 1969, American troop presence in the region had peaked around 543,000.[2] Yet, by all estimations, America had still been playing a supporting role in the fight between the North and the South.

The second war really began when the Americans got deeply involved (militarily of course) in Vietnam. The American government gradually increased its military presence in Southeast Asia. Between 1965 and 1968, American troops in Vietnam grew from approximately 180,000 to over 500,000. According to several official and non-official sources, including reputable news organizations, more than 2.5 million Americans served in the conflict.[3] All the same, there were 2,646 American service members listed as Prisoner of War (POW) or Missing in Action (MIA).[4]

THE EFFECTS OF THE WAR

To this day, the remnants of the Vietnam War are still echoing in the United States. Many families are still reeling from the effects of the conflict. As of April 10, 2015, approximately, 1,677 soldiers are still missing in Vietnam.[5] A war that was supposed to be easy, to the limit of the American military of course, turned out to be extremely complicated and costly for the Americans, primarily for their military personnel.

While American soldiers struggled in the Vietnam jungle, a group of fighters, known as the *"Viet Cong,"*[6] ambushed them and inflicted considerable damages to both their physics and mental states. The American military cunning and might, which include its superiority in the air and at sea, were no use in the guerrilla warfare, which had been orchestrated by the Viet Cong Forces.

The effects of the war were palpable both in the jungle of Vietnam and at home. The war was taking a toll on the morale of the troops. The sheer brutality of the fighting and the degree of the carnage that embroiled the American military forces were insurmountable. Resultantly, many American fighters could not bear the full breadth of the effects of the war.

At home, the situation was even more precarious. Disgruntled Americans started to protest against the war. The public did not understand the reason American soldiers, including relatives (e.g., husbands, wives, sons, and daughters) and innocent civilians, had to die in Vietnam. The war became very unpopular. The civilian death toll was also incalculable. Although there were some staunch supporters that found themselves on the fringe of the conflict, by early 1970s, most Americans simply refused to validate the war.

Before the war ended, many people lost their lives, including military and civilians. It is estimated that approximately 1 million people died in Vietnam. In total, there were approximately 1.3 million deaths, which include the casualties sustained by the other countries involved in the conflict. In addition, more than 58,000 American service members died in Vietnam; that number also includes both combatants and non-combatants.[7]

Most observers agree that Vietnam was the result of an ill-conceived foreign policy. This war was not within the reach of the American military. This was neither their war to fight nor their war to win. The Americans got involved in Vietnam without a clear understanding as to what they could get out of it. Vietnam was a punitive war and the Americans were humiliated in Indochina, just to put it in a lesser pejorative term.

THE DEMISE OF AMERICAN POLITICIANS

Since the Americans inherited the Vietnam War, they allied with the South Vietnamese regime. By that time, the French had been defeated and, for the most part, they had abandoned Indochina or parts of it. Subsequently, the Americans poised their selves as the sole guarantors of the French imperialist legacy in Southeast Asia.

The French were not necessarily fighting for a particular cause in Vietnam. But it appears that the French had been defending their rights to control Vietnamese territory. It could also be said that in the beginning, America had no ideological framework for its involvement in Indochina.

The Vietnam War did not fall within the realm of traditional fights to preserve American interests in that part of the world. Little by little, however, it became clear that America had a different doctrinal reason for being in Vietnam. In that sense, the rationale for the American involvement in Indochina could be understood within the realm of the notion commonly known as the *"Containment Doctrine."* This was a policy approach specifically designed to prevent nations, such as the Soviet Union (now Russia) and China, from expanding their influence in Southeast Asia.[8]

Based on the above understanding, the popular belief is that America sought to prevent the rise of Communist influence in Indochina in particular. Vietnam was certainly one of the many places in Southeast Asia, which the Americans would seek to impede the Chinese and the Soviets from taking a hold or from exerting any influence. Beyond recall, this was the case both politically and militarily. However, in an attempt to achieve that goal, American officials, not to mention a number of innocent civilians and military personnel on both sides of the conflict, when all is said and done, paid an enormous price.

At the time, most American politicians believed that America was the sole moral authority in the world. But this worldview was not shared, of necessity, by ordinary Americans. Still, it was certainly a *de facto viewpoint* during that epoch. Moreover, it could be said that this view was putatively based on the notion that America was to become the guardian of the world. This worldview was rooted on ideas akin to the notion of *Manifest Destiny.*[9]

It could further be said that the American involvement in Indochina was guided by several other doctrinal precepts as well. One of such doctrinal approaches could be understood as the Truman Doctrine.[10] In that sense, it could also be echoed [with confidence of course] that the Vietnam War had been fought within a similar context.

Despite the ideological underpinnings of the American presence in Southeast Asia, the war was very unpopular. But the public repudiation of the war could be understood as a disavowal of the same doctrinal approach that made *"America great"* in the eyes of so many American politicians. It was as if those who opposed the war were anti-America in their core belief systems. But this view was often echoed during this period in order to describe those who opposed the war.

I am not suggesting that everyone opposed the war for the same reasons. But one core issue that seemed to resound (at times very loud) against the war is that Vietnam was not America's war. For the most part, the American public refuted their government's presence in Indochina.

In contrast to the political tide at the time, many people did not seem to agree with the notion that the United States had an obligation to play a role in that part of the world. Vietnam was a war engendered by American politicians for all the wrong reasons, some might say. This war was not perforce engendered in the country's interest as a whole. Hence, the American people had no qualm refuting the war.

At some point, the American government had little or no other options but to reduce its military presence in Indochina. From that understanding, the war was supposed to end. But politicians found a way to continue fighting the Vietnam War by proxy.

A SURROGATE WAR

In 1973, the Nixon administration declared that the Vietnam War had officially ended. The problem is that it did not seem like there was a true intention on the American side to end the conflict. There was no clear understanding as to the extent to which the American government would still support the South Vietnamese regime beyond that point.

Equally, there were no set dates as to when and how the American military would begin withdrawing from the region. The declaration made by President Nixon seemed to have had little or no immediate effects in the conflict. While in theory the war officially ended, there were fighting incidents involving American military personnel. But for the most part, the roles had been reversed.

It is true that the Americans were supporting the French in Vietnam. But when the American public rejected their government's involvement in the conflict, the South Vietnamese regime became America's surrogate military arms in the region. In essence, the war was still ongoing. But the battles were mostly relegated to South Vietnamese fighters.

In theory, there is no doubt that American troops officially withdrew from Vietnam in 1973. But from a practical standpoint, it should also be pointed out that the American military was still embroiled in the conflict. In many parts of Vietnam, the war was still ongoing, even after it had been declared to end.

There is an argument to be made that the United States had been stuck in Vietnam. By that time, South Vietnam was somewhat a representative of the American government in the region. In this regard, the South Vietnamese regime was a political façade for the Americans in Indochina. But with regards to the above-mentioned reality, it seems that, even after 1973, Vietnam was still America's war to either win or lose.

It is undeniable that the American military was trapped in Vietnam. It was a war, which America could not easily end, depart from, or avoid its implications. Despite the official declaration that the war ended, American soldiers were still involved in hostilities throughout the region. After 1973, for instance, Vietnam became a surrogate war, which had been fought, at least on the surface, by South Vietnamese fighters. But under the radar, the Americans were still guiding war efforts.

During that period, there were constant skirmishes between American soldiers and North Vietnamese forces. See casualty figures after 1973 on the Defense casualty analysis system's website to learn more.[11] In any event, there were constant clashes between South and North Vietnamese fighters. This is the reason the American government still had a stake in the outcome of the conflict, even though the American President himself had officially declared that America was no longer part of the war. This may also explain the reason funding the South Vietnamese regime was quintessential.

ABANDONING THE GVN (SOUTH VIETNAM)

In a sudden twist of events, in the spring of 1975, the American government withdrew its remaining personnel all across Vietnam, which included both military and civilian staff members. Of course, by that time, there were not many American fighters left on the ground. The American military presence had been dwindling since 1973. But as noted earlier, Vietnam was still America's war.

There was a significant amount of individuals, whom solidified the American presence is some specific parts of Indochina, including in Vietnam itself. It is true that many of these people were prisoners of war. But America still had a reason to be in Vietnam.

The problem is that America was divided about the war. The division was very deep. That division was not just based on a mere refusal to endorse one's country in a war, which had been very devastating and very costly in both materials and in human lives. The country was divided at its core.

Vietnam had become a cancer in American society. The political existence of the country itself was threatened. Social order was in peril. For some politicians, they had to do something to change the course of the war. By that time, there were fewer alternatives for an honorable end of the conflict.

Perhaps the least complicated option was to leave the GVN (or the Government of South Vietnam) on its own and to fend for itself. But at this point, America had no choice but to abandon its most valuable ally. In this instance, it was the South Vietnamese regime itself.

As we will examine in more detail in this document, the American government ultimately ordered the evacuation of embassy personnel in Saigon. That event led to an exodus of people who were trying to leave the region. Perhaps this particular event was not anticipated, at least on the American side. But this situation convincingly conveyed the imagery that the Americans were running away from North Vietnamese fighters.

America also left behind a few military personnel in Vietnam. To this day, more than sixteen hundred Americans are still missing in Vietnam. In other words, there is no closure in the Vietnam Conflict. The abrupt departure from the region was indicative that both American military and civilian officials did not plan to leave Vietnam the manner that they did.

We must determine why the American government espoused a sudden change of policy direction. That is to say, we must decipher the reason this reversal policy had been adopted in this particular juncture. Let us explore the conflict a bit further.

A Tough War

Vietnam And Military History

CHAPTER SIX

6. A Complex Military Conflict

VIETNAM WAS AN EXTREMELY complicated military conflict. The fighting itself was very unorthodox. Daily scuffles between the American military and the Viet Cong Army were laden with an array of variables. The majority of the fighting took place in unusual settings.

For the most part, military combats occurred in jungle-like settings, i.e., in places where airplanes, guided missiles, and helicopters had little or no lasting effects on the enemy. The fights also spilled over in many locations, notably in various parts of Indochina. But battles did not take place in one particular area; the combat zone was everywhere.

The enemies did not have a specific trait or a characteristic. Any person could be an enemy fighter. That is to say, Vietnam was not a conventional war.

In the forest of Laos and Cambodia, many American fighters sustained heavy casualties. These places were rigged with booby traps and other landmines. In other situations, military clashes occurred in urban areas, including in cities and towns.

In these places, it was almost impossible to distinguish enemy fighters from the civilian population. In many instances, the Viet Cong army used members of the local population, including women and children, as human shields. As a result, they inflicted a considerable amount of blows to the Americans.

Viet Cong forces were relentless and ruthless in their attacks against the American military. They regularly detonated improvised explosives and other types of homemade bombs, which, in many situations, inflicted considerable damages to both human lives and properties. Viet Cong fighters frequently launched surprised attacks on American military bases, oftentimes, at night. These attacks targeted places where American soldiers habitually *"hangout"* or places where huge crowds gathered.

These types of attacks time and again occurred in nightclubs, supermarkets, restaurants, or other places, which had been heavily frequented by the public. That also included places that most Americans (i.e., both military and civilians) visited on a regular basis. The effects of such sneaky attacks were incommensurable. These tactics affected the psychological well-being of most American soldiers. But these attacks inflicted enormous emotional damages to Vietnamese citizens as well.

Fighting also occurred in villages or remote terrains. But the Viet Cong army had the upper hand in these fights due to their familiarity of the landscape. In some instances, fighting incidents occurred in tunnels. Those tunnels were designed specifically to wreak havoc on American forces.[1]

These tunnels consisted of a network of small access holes, approximately 2 feet wide and 3 feet deep. The tunnels had a symbolic significance to Viet Cong fighters; they believe that these passageways would help them, at least in the end, win the war.[2] These small, but important, advantages provided an irrefutable military edge to North Vietnamese fighters.

Many enemy fighters had little or no familiarity with firearms.[3] Yet, that was not a handicap for the Viet Cong army. Viet Cong men were extremely motivated and dedicated fighters.[4] They preferred guerrilla-type warfare; they also preferred guerilla weaponry.[5] Guerilla weapons were lightweight and compact; they were also versatile. They could be used for jungle fighting and they were perfect to use in the tunnels. In addition, these weapons were easily concealed for covert transportation.[6]

The American military, on the other hand, had to adjust to the reality of being in Vietnam. For example, one of the most frightening aspects of the battleground is that most American fighters were not familiar with the topography of the land. They were neither equipped nor trained for the kind of warfare they encountered in the jungles of Cambodia and Laos.

Age was an important factor on the battlefield; it is worth pointing out here as well. Many American soldiers were very young; they had not really fought in similar types of conflicts before. Their exposure to urban-style battles had been extremely limited or non-existent. The jungle of Vietnam had left many soldiers with a bitter memory, which could not be erased by time alone. The problem is that most American soldiers had to find a means to cope with the reality of fighting a war that they might not win.

The Objectification Of Fighters

Vietnam was not just a military venture; it was also akin to a social theater. The battlegrounds were drawn along the lines of political, social/cultural, and even economic ideologies. From an ideological standpoint, the Americans sought to impose their intrinsic views of the world onto the Vietnamese people. They sought to bring civilization to the region, at least from their vantage point.

It would not be farfetched to state that most people in Vietnam saw the Americans as an occupying force. A number of Vietnamese did not seem to care much for American idealism. It could also be said that most Vietnamese saw the Americans as occupiers. North Vietnamese fighters almost certainly viewed American soldiers as foreigners and destroyers.

The argument could be made that most Northern fighters were convinced that the Americans were devoid of humanity. From their vantage point, these soldiers had no understanding of the Vietnamese culture. Conceivably, the degree of North Vietnamese hatred for the Americans was very deep. Perhaps that might explain the reason these fighters fought against the Americans so relentlessly.

What I am saying is that Viet Cong fighters probably saw American soldiers as the worst alternative to the French. From what could be discerned at the time, these fighters were extremely motivated. They were also determined to prevent any form of American control in Indochina.

There is a cultural factor worth pointing out as well. As inferred above, the Vietnamese people were a little bit on the opposite side of the cultural spectrum with the Americans. From this viewpoint, the Vietnamese way of life, their society, and culture did not weigh much in the battle scale, at least not to outward appearances. But the Americans also saw nonconformist dissidents as savages. They believed that such individuals needed to be taught democratic ideals.

From a political standpoint, the Americans sought to obliterate any dissenting voice in Vietnam. The Americans decided the individuals who should be in charge of the country. They also chose the people who should rule the region, including both national and local leaders. It seemed as though the Vietnamese people had little or no say in their own political destiny. Perhaps this reality infused a sense of nationalism in many North Vietnamese fighters.

Just as the French had done before, the Americans poised themselves as the sole entity that could determine the political future of Vietnam. American officials sought to bar any alternatives to what they offered, including a path towards Communism. But it did not appear that most Vietnamese people wanted to be under American control.

At the time, several Vietnamese seemed to prefer Communism to Capitalism. Still, there was a sense that the Vietnamese people were political aliens on their own land and had no self-determination. This reality was simply unacceptable for a number of people in Vietnam.

DEHUMANIZING VIETNAMESE FIGHTERS

Another aspect of the Vietnam Conflict is worth reiterating here as well. Most Vietnamese dissidents were subjugated to a status of infrahuman.[7] Their lives did not seem to worth as much as other lives, including American lives. Various photos taken during the war depicted the extent to which the lives of Vietnamese fighters were devalued.[8]

Several images illustrated how South Vietnam armed forces callously killed both armed rebels and civilians. Some of these images are very graphic. The objectification of the Vietnamese people was unequivocal; that reality was apparent throughout the conflict. But a number of factors also made the war an exceptional military venture in both countries' history.

It could be said that Vietnam was a war of pride. The Americans did not want to lose the war, even though they knew (or perhaps they had reasons to know) that they could not win it. Vietnamese fighters, on the other hand, were unyielding, even though it was apparent that they were being consumed by the war itself. Thus, Vietnam was a fight to the death on both sides.

Somehow, the Americans had to back down; they could not accomplish their ultimate goal of containing the Soviet Union and China in the region. They could not even contain North Vietnamese fighters.

The Vietnam Conflict was ostensibly driven by misguided ideologies and misapprehensions.[9] I would also say that the war was sustained by a foolish pride (on both sides) to fight until the end. Of course, this is just a hunch. But assuming that this was indeed the case, beyond the shadow of doubt, it would, explain some of the atrocities that transpired during the hostilities.

The war was a difficult time for the Vietnamese people. The majority of the population had become the victims of the desires of those who seemed unaffected by their suffering. In some cases, entire villages were disseminated by both Vietnamese fighters and American soldiers. The civilian population had been caught in the crossfire.

THE REAL VICTIMS

The war had led to a number of unconscionable acts in Indochina. Many of these atrocities had been committed by all the parties involved. In other words, it was carnage on both ends, to say the least.

The most demoralizing aspect of the war was the fact that the civilian population suffered enormously from the fighting. They were victimized by the actions posed by both the Americans and the Vietnamese military. On the Vietnamese side, there were no clear distinctions between Northern (e.g., Vietcong) rebels and South Vietnamese fighters. But the Americans were also victimized.

For some reasons, most outside observers expressed little sympathy for the Americans. Of course, they recognized that American soldiers sustained a considerable amount of casualties in the conflict. But a few incidents provided credence to the notion that the Americans were the bad people [i.e., the bad guys] in this horrendous play or this despicable horror movie. One particular event shook the world's consciousness, even though there were numerous attempts to hide the truth. It was the My Lai Massacre and the official cover-up that ensued.[10]

During that unfortunate episode, several American military personnel apparently slaughtered as many as 500 people in a village in South Vietnam known as My Lai.[11] In the early spring of 1968 (in the month of March to be precise), it is believed that a number of American soldiers brutally massacred men, women, children, and even elderly people in that remote village. It is also believed that after the incident, American officials tried to distort the version of the events.

Nobody denied the American involvement in the massacre. However, the extent of the cover-up that ensued is not well understood. But it is quasi certain that there is enough evidence to suggest a cover-up attempt. One might say that there was a deliberate endeavor on the part of the American military to muffle to truth in My Lai.

It must be noted that, to this day, the motive for the May Lai carnage still eludes most historians. Nevertheless, it is widely believed that low troop morale was at the roots of the event itself.[12] Some observers have even contended that perhaps combat-related stress and fatigue could be somewhat responsible for the degree of rage and the complete disregard for human lives, which members of the American military displayed in My Lai.

Over the years, many observers have disputed several accounts regarding the way American soldiers conducted themselves in Vietnam. But other commentators have also casted doubts about the degree to which American troops deserve the blame for the many lost of lives in the war itself. After all, North Vietnamese fighters often used the local population as human shields.

The point is that American soldiers were not alone in the sheer brutality and the degree of inhumanity that had been perpetrated against the civilian population in Vietnam. It was commonly known that the strategy of the Vietcong army was to use the civilian population as bait and even as weapons. Their level of indifference towards the lives of the Vietnamese people was unconscionable. What was also certain is that the American military displayed a level of brutality that astounded most observers during the Vietnam War.

UNABLE TO COPE

The age factor is also relevant to reiterate in this instance. For the most part, American fighters were not familiar with this kind of war. For many American soldiers, Vietnam was their first exposure to real fighting. Not surprisingly, many young American men died in Vietnam. Approximately 61% of the men killed in Vietnam were 21 and younger.[13]

Those who survived the conflict have been damaged beyond repair. Some of them are scarred both physically and emotionally. As a result, many of these young soldiers could not cope with the sheer brutality of the fighting or the memory thereof. Some used drugs or all sorts of substances in order to find a means to cope with the ghosts of Vietnam. Some of them did not (or simply could not) make it.

A number of American soldiers committed suicide both during and after the Vietnam War. The National archive lists 382 deaths as self-inflicted during the war.[14] But it must be noted that the exact number of Vietnam-related suicides, notably after the conflict ended, is often disputed.

The New York Times, for instance, looked at a report from the Center for Disease Control, which placed the number of Vietnam-related suicides among veterans around 9,000. [15] But other estimates placed that number at a higher proportion. Susan Donaldson James, for example, listed that there were more than 100,000 suicide-related deaths between 1999 and 2010 by Vietnam War veterans.[16]

To this day, Vietnam-related disabilities are also high in the United States military. It is believed that the number of Vietnam-related injuries exceeded the number of combat-related wounds from previous wars, including the Second World War. [17] For example, Vietnam-related amputation or crippling wounds, which chiefly occur in lower extremities, were 300% higher from the Vietnam War than both World War II and the Korean War.[18]

At the highest point of the conflict, anti-war activists were constantly protesting the war. At home, support for the war had been dwindling at an astronomical pace. As the number of American casualties mounted and the war seemed to drag-on for an indefinite time, the American people became disenchanted with their country's military pursuit in the region. Many people took to the streets to vent their disagreements with the war. Vietnam became the most unpopular war in American history.

These protests, in turn, pitted law enforcement with the citizenry. Daily television broadcasts were filled with images of young people who were confronting the police in the streets. There were many skirmishes on college campuses across America. Television newscasts also paraded images of death and destruction throughout Vietnam. The war had a devastating effect at home. The war created a rift in American society, which, to this day, is still profound.

WINDING DOWN THE WAR

After many years of fighting, there was no clear victory in sight. Most Americans did not know the reason the war was being fought. There was no comprehensible strategy to subdue the Northern rebels. There were no clear political or military objectives for a swift victory in Vietnam.

That being noted, I imagine that the previous argument would be accurate only when speaking about the American military. Evidently, it was a different story for the North Vietnamese military. Although they were fragmentized, they had a unified mission. They had to rebuff the enemy.

My point is that, North Vietnamese fighters, in many cases, seemed to have a clear goal in mind. They wanted to rid their country of foreign dominion. But on the American side, that kind of motivation was simply not there. Vietnam was not the American military's war.

The fighting created a sense of hopelessness on the American side. That reality, in turn, affected troop morale. This fact might also explain the reason many American service members committed suicide both during and after the conflict. As noted in the previous segment, the amount of post war-related trauma was significant on the American side.

The complexity of the military fighting did not only stem from the rigidity of the environment and the nature of the war itself. Most policy makers did not seem to have a specific strategy to win in Vietnam. A reasonable argument is that the war had been fought on chimerical ideals or on unachievable goals. Since the initial stage of the fighting, many observers viewed the conflict as a lost cause.

The argument is that, most American leaders, including military and civilian officials, did not seem to have a clear ideal for engaging the country in the war. Arguably, the Vietnam War was the brainchild of politicians who believed that America's place in the world was to police every other nation within it. As insinuated in anterior segments, this war was the result of worldviews that considered America as the only blessed land on earth.

Unmistakably, the understanding during the time of the American involvement in Southeast Asia was one-sided. Nonetheless, many politicians believed that America had an ordained duty to disseminate American values throughout the world. For the most part, U.S. foreign policies were tailored to reflect that worldview. But this was a view of the world that was put into question, if not completely refuted, in Vietnam.

Regardless of the nature of the American idealism within the Indochina region, for a number of people in Vietnam, Laos, and Cambodia, the war was an important fight for their own survival. They had been invaded, occupied, and turned into subjects on their own land by a powerful nation (i.e., France). Now, they were fighting to prevent an even more powerful nation—in this instance, the United States—from subjugating them to ideals that were not necessarily compatible with their views of the world. Justifiably, losing the war was not an option for many Viet Cong fighters.

CHAPTER SEVEN

7. LONG-TERM EFFECTS OF THE WAR

BY THE EARLY 1970s, the effects of the conduct of the Vietnam War were the subject of intense political debates. As it were, in Washington, at least during the initial months, supports for the war were based on a bipartisan approach. But it must be noted that political supports for the war during that time were mostly apparent along ideological lines.

Most politicians, particularly on the conservative side (e.g., Republicans), were fond of the war. By contrast, many liberals (e.g., Democrats) tended to be against it. In spite of that reality, however, it could also be said that there was a sense of a political unification to enter the conflict militarily.

It must also be echoed that many observers had mixed feelings about the war. Still, there was a palpable sense of patriotism whenever policy makers spoke about Vietnam. Despite the many disagreements that impregnated the political discourse at home, few people wanted to see America lose in Vietnam.

From a multinational standpoint, participation to the war was relatively feeble. Of course, countries that were allies to the United States on other fronts also supported the American presence in Vietnam. But from a broader perspective, most observers had mixed feelings about the war.

On the surface, few people in the world seemed convinced of the necessity of the conflict. An even lesser amount of observers viewed war efforts in positive terms. Thus, there were little or no foreign supports for the American involvement in Indochina; at least this was the case towards the end of the conflict.

What I am saying here is that worldwide supports for Vietnam were relatively meager. A number of countries were silent about the war. Few joined forces to help American troops on the ground. But most American enemies or potential enemies regarded Vietnam as a laboratory to learn new tricks and techniques about America's war-fighting strategies.

It would not be exaggerated to say that, during the war, several *"Would-be-American-foes"* learned how to fight America. Yes, the United States had a lot of firepower. But its military might was no match for the many urban fights (e.g., street fighting) that ensued.

The American military was ill prepared to engage the enemy on its own turf, while battling in guerrilla fights. Vietnam proved to be a dangerous battleground for American fighters; this was true, I would say; no matter how one frames the debate.

A similar scenario was clearly repeated in later wars, which the American military participated or instigated. For example, both the wars in Afghanistan (2001) and Iraq (2003) could illustrate this assertion a bit further. These two wars could be considered as reminiscent of the Vietnam Conflict.

In Iraq, for instance, the parallel was astounding.[1] A score of American soldiers died because of enemy booby traps/ambushes or improvised weaponry. Some observers noted that the use of explosive gadgets such as IEDs (also known as Improvised Explosive Devices) was somewhat akin to the kinds of explosive North Vietnamese fighters used to detonate.

This understanding is on par with the idea that Vietnam was very lethal for the American military. Unlike previous conflicts, this war was fought in a jungle-like setting. It was a sort of urban-style warfare to say the least. There is no doubt that Vietnam was very different from World War II. This was particularly evident in terms of the types of military clashes that took place there. Up until that point, American soldiers were not accustomed to that kind of warfare. Hence, the reason Vietnam was a punitive war.

Most American soldiers struggled to get a handle of the fighting. They also made great efforts in order to find their footing in the unforgiving jungles of Laos and Cambodia. But it is fair to say that the Americans never really found the right tactic to win the war or the appropriate strategy to conquer Vietnam, not to mention Southeast Asia. It was a complete failure.

DIVERGENT VIEWS ABOUT VIETNAM

In America, views are predominantly disconcerted about the nature of the conflict. Most people do not agree as to the reason the war started. In the same way, few people agree as to the reason the war ended. In that sense, inquiring about the nature of the conflict averred to be a tedious project.

The arguments echoed throughout this volume center on the premise that the war ended prematurely. The presumption is the Americans wanted to control Indochina. But their ultimate goal was to prevent the spread of Communism in Southeast Asia in particular. But when they left the region, Communism seemingly became the norm in that part of the world, as Communist North reunited with the South.

In view of this reality, one plausible inference worth pointing out here is that America's most livid fear for Southeast Asia did not concretize. The fall of Vietnam into the hands of North Vietnamese fighters did not have a domino effect, just like many policy makers [mostly Americans] had predicted. Southeast Asia (i.e., Indochina as a whole) did not descend in some chaotic scenery of socialist revolutions. But the same could not be said about the American government. The war left several governmental agencies in a state of hysteria.

Nonetheless, a number of questions regarding the conflict are left unanswered. For example, what went wrong in Vietnam? What went wrong in Washington? "The rapid demise of South Vietnam boded ill for the United States," many observers echoed.[2] There was a blame game within the American government regarding who should be held responsible for the Vietnam debacle.

There is no question that North Vietnam played a military role in driving the South to the brink of collapse.[3] But as previously illustrated, the culprit often identified by most observers is the United States Congress itself (*See* Blaming Congress). The argument is that Congress singlehandedly led to the collapse of Nguyen Van Thieu's regime on April 1975.[4]

The pervading belief is that South Vietnam was still a viable entity up until its ultimate demise and collapse.[5] The view often echoed in the literature is that, the American legislative branch (on its own of course) weakened the South Vietnamese regime. In the same vein, the position widely held in American politics is that Congress ended the conflict. It did so unilaterally. But to what degree this understanding is accurate? Let us explore.

ENDING THE WAR

The Vietnam War ended in a not so uplifting manner. On April 23, 1975, President Gerald Ford declared the end of American hostilities in Vietnam. This was the second declaration made by an American President regarding the Vietnam Conflict.

In theory, President Richard Nixon ended the war two years prior (1973). But in practice, President Ford's decision is the one that had the most relevance. This was part of a series of final executive acts to end the American presence in Indochina.

Without a doubt, the month of April marked the end of the Vietnam Conflict. The last remaining American military personal left the region during that month. To that extent, it could be adumbrated that the decision announced by President Ford was not the original policy choice that the government had sought to implement in the conflict.

History has shown that America did not want to relinquish its control over the region to Communist ideologues. Until the last minutes, American policy makers fought relentlessly to prevent such a fate. Still, the salient question is why the war subsequently ended the manner that it did.

A plausible argument is that America was forced out of the region. I understand that this view is not unanimous. I also reckon that most people believe that America ended the war on its own volition. This is roundly true; I would admit it.

From a military angle, one might contend that America did not lose the war per se. But on that premise, it must also be pointed out that the American military had sustained considerable amount of casualties in the process of fighting the war. Thus, Vietnam was not an easy war for the Americans; at least, the conflict itself was far from the type of military exchange that they might have anticipated.

By all accounts, Vietnamese forces sustained more military losses than the Americans did (*See* Chapter 4). The brutality of the fighting was unequivocal. From these considerations alone, one could exclaim that America's exit from the region was not the result of a military campaign by North Vietnamese fighters.

The reason for the forced exit evoked here is mostly the result of self-inflicted wounds. But whatever the issues the Ford administration faced, they were mostly internal. In all probability, the problem was created by American policy makers who seemed unable to come to a consensus over Vietnam.

THE VIETNAMIZATION OF THE WAR

As debated in previous sections, Congress has always been regarded as the major force behind the collapse of South Vietnam. The view often echoed in various circles—and inexorably shared in most Washington's political alleys and corridors—is that South Vietnam was carrying its own weight. The belief is that since the United States signed an agreement in Paris, which is known as the *"Paris agreement,"* American troops were shielded from the fighting.

The popular view is that the Americans had successfully shifted the military responsibilities of the war onto the South Vietnamese regime. As a result, the American military had considerably dialed down its involvement in the fighting. Even so, most observers regarded the Paris accord as an ephemeras truce, which did not last long enough to prevent further hostilities.[6]

At first sight, the Americans were right in the middle of the fighting. In other words, Vietnam was still America's war. To that degree, it must be reiterated that, at the time, the South Vietnamese regime was obviously acting as a surrogate party for the American government in the conflict.

Many people in Washington argued that the Paris agreement had proved that the South Vietnamese regime had the capacity to engage the enemy and assume the responsibility of fighting against the North.[7] The so-called *"Vietnamization"* of the conflict was working, as echoed by President Richard Nixon himself.[8] The contention often echoed by proponents of the war is that, by refusing to approve military aid to Thieu's regime, Congress precipitated North Vietnamese aggression, which, at the last moment, led to the collapse of South Vietnam.[9]

Paradoxically, both possibilities could not be true. The United States could not have been forced out of Vietnam, at the same time, it could not be said that American officials left the region based on their assessment of the situation. From this angle, I would reiterate that Congress could not be the only entity that deserves the blame for the premature end of the conflict. Other actors played a role in weakening the American government in Vietnam.

The White House, for instance, often acted indecisively and hesitated to make the critical decisions at necessary times.[10] There was reluctance on the part of Richard Nixon, Gerald Ford, and Henry Kissinger, the foreign policy advisor at the time, to acknowledge the inevitable. To put it in a simpler term, "Congress had to accept the responsibilities that went along with the ineluctable end to the nation's involvement in Southeast Asia between 1974 and 1975."[11]

After all said and done, the Legislature had to act. Refusing military funding to the South Vietnam regime was clearly the only avenue for Congress to put its foot down and convey the unequivocal message that the United States could no longer be part of the Vietnam Conflict. It is conceivable that this was the reason most members of Congress acted in the manner that they did.

My point is that it is important to delineate the line between the policy reason the war ended and the political struggle that led to the adoption of such a policy. It is also paramount to examine the extent to which politics informed the American governmental policy initiatives in Vietnam. Of course, I suppose that it could be difficult to delineate between policy and politics, particularly when it comes to transnational issues. But as echoed throughout this document, we could definitely speculate from here and out.

It is true that the line between the two concepts is blurry. Still, we could examine the conflict from two separate plane fields. Thus, Vietnam could be understood as a two-dimensional war.

A TWO-DIMENSIONAL WAR

The Vietnam War had two dimensions. The war was being fought on two different grounds. On the one hand, there was a political war. This war was fought in Washington. This war was mostly motivated by political ideologies. On the other hand, however, there was the actual war. This war was being fought on ground zero. In this instance, I am referring to Vietnam itself. It could also be said that this war was mostly fought by pride.

The war was lost at home long before it was lost in Vietnam. By the time the United States decided to pull out its troops from the region, the war had already been lost at home. All the events that transpired between April 1 and April 30, 1975 were symbolic in nature. The fate of the war had already been sealed. When Congress refused to approve emergency funding, as requested by the Nixon administration, the war officially ended.

My point is that when President Ford made the request for additional funding for South Vietnam and that request was not approved, this was proof that there was no political desire in Washington to grant the President his wishes. Belatedly, President Ford had fewer alternatives, but to withdraw from the region. His hands were tied up. Then again, that is just a hunch. We need to go deeper in the issues in order to understand the nature of the withdrawal decision itself.

There were moments towards the end of the conflict, which suggest that the American government had lost its footing in Vietnam. The epic American embassy evacuation from Saigon, for instance, could be understood as a frantic move on the part of President Ford to avoid the worst outcome in the region. The President surely knew that he did not benefit the support of Congress to continue maintaining a U.S. military presence in Vietnam. This decision was among the last events of the war.

The images of Marine helicopters landing on rooftops to rescue stranded Americans and other Vietnamese supporters conveyed the unequivocal message that America was on the run. When the United States Congress rejected the request for military aid to the South Vietnamese regime, it became unequivocal that the government was in a frenzy state. If we were to look at the issues only from this angle, it might become very hard to convince observers that America had won the war.

It seems evident that the American evacuation from the Vietnamese capital (i.e., Saigon) symbolized that the war had officially ended. In the next few chapters, I will examine the policy rationale that led to this infamous end. I will examine the reason for this sudden policy change in the region. I will also examine the extent to which politics dictated the last hours of the war or the degree to which the withdrawal was part of a well-calculated strategy.

But before we get to that point, let us explore the after effects of the Vietnam debacle. Let us revisit the political ramifications of the conflict itself. Let us examine how American politicians were affected by Vietnam.

CHAPTER EIGHT

8. VIETNAM AS A LITMUS TEST

WHEN PRESIDENT GERALD FORD ordered the evacuation of American Embassy personnel from Saigon, the reactions at home were mitigated. At the time, this particular embassy was considered the last American stronghold in Indochina. That decision surely brought jubilation to some Americans (e.g., anti-war activists); but it also brought a sense of consternation to others.

The decision to evacuate Vietnam seemed to have emanated from a larger policy framework. In order to understand the rationale that guided the withdrawal decision itself, I utilize a conceptual framework, which had been proposed by Graham T. Allison. I will discuss the models in length in chapters thirteen through sixteen. The present chapter evaluates some of the issues that resulted from the sudden change of policy in Indochina.

The models were developed as a means to examine the *Cuban Missile Crisis* in 1962. Allison developed three models. But here, I only used two of the models. Chapter 15 discusses the application of the models to Vietnam at length.

My contention is that the United States was forced out of Vietnam. But let me point out that I relied solely on my understanding of the models in order to intimate what transpired, as the case may be, at the governmental level.

My primary goal is to cater a greater appreciation of what took place in Washington from a policy-making standpoint. But another objective is to examine the role of politics within the agencies that were in charge of the conduct of the war. Such agencies might include, but might not be limited to, the legislative and executive branches of government.

A tertiary goal is to link American policy-making rituals to the withdrawal decision. It is also important to take into account other aspects about the war. Thus, it is essential to examine the domestic dissonance and the social upheaval, which had been growing at home.

In sum, it is important to examine the salient arguments, which are regularly echoed in the literature regarding the reason the Vietnam War ended. In that spirit, it is quintessential to touch upon some of the diplomatic demarches, which had been undertaken by the American government in order to reach out to the Vietnamese regime. It is also of the rigor to assess the degree to which the remnants of the Vietnam War are still relevant in American politics today. The next section will do just that.

UNDERSTANDING THE VIETNAM CONFLICT

The Vietnam Conflict has left an indelible mark on the psyche of those who participated in that military theater. This war has also left a scar in American foreign policy in Asia.[1] The most memorable impact of the war could be best explored from the lens of domestic politics. With that knowledge in mind, it is important to revisit the degree to which internal issues affected foreign policy initiatives.

An unintended consequence of the conflict is that citizen trust in their government had eroded considerably. [2] Because of Vietnam, fewer Americans trust their government to do the right thing, particularly when it comes to foreign conflicts. But this is mostly apparent when it comes to the adoption of policies, which might commit the nation in military skirmishes abroad. The presumption is that politicians would do anything or would say anything to get the American government involved in global conflicts.

Another source of anger in American society is that politicians seldom suffer from the outcomes of their own decisions. In many cases, the American people are forced to pay for the consequences of ill-advised decision or actions taken by ideologically driven politicians. This view could be understood as the after effects of the war. It could also be said that Vietnam transcended the way the American people view the role of their government in world affairs.

The conflict has had a larger impact on public sentiments about wars in general. Since the Vietnam fiasco, most Americans have begun to question the role the country's military should play in global affairs. Here, I am referring to planetary skirmishes that do not significantly involve an American interest. But before Vietnam and even during the conflict itself, this was a completely different story.

To this day, the effects of the decision to commit American troops into the conflict continue to influence domestic politics in many ways. For instance, because of Vietnam, fewer Americans are willing to hand government officials a blank check, which would allow them to commit the country in any conflict they might desire.

Other unintended consequences are worth exploring here as well. Few people (notably politicians) could hide their past during the Vietnam era, especially if they engaged in some questionable conducts during the war. Some observers have labeled this reality as a *curse* in American foreign politics. That curse, for lack of a better term, is often linked directly to the Vietnam collapse itself. Let us explore the nature of that curse a bit further.

THE CURSE OF VIETNAM

There is no question about it; the Vietnam Conflict had divided the American people. The political class also suffered from a credibility deficiency because of the war. This military adventure did more damage to the American political class than any wars before it. The so-called *"The curse of Vietnam"* has never left American politics.[3]

Questions regarding politicians who avoided (i.e., dodged) going to war have always been the subject of sensational debates. Many American presidents [including people who held public office or those who sought such offices] have been satirized for avoiding the call of service in Vietnam. Some are derided for their attempt to snub the military draft (or other military service requirements).

Former President George W. Bush, for instance, is often the subject of invasive inquiries, if not derision, for joining the National Guard. Many people viewed this move as a deliberate attempt on the part of Mr. Bush to escape the possibility of going to Vietnam.[4] Other political figures are derided for obtaining student deferments as a means to avoid going to

Vietnam. Among these politicians are former Senator [former Vice President] Joseph R. Biden Jr., and former Vice President Dick Cheney.

Vice President Cheney, for instance, obtained five draft deferments during the Vietnam War. [5] This aspect of Mr. Cheney's past was the subject of an intense scrutiny during the 2004 presidential campaign. Former Vice President Joseph Biden also received a similar number of drafts during Vietnam.[6]

A number of prominent political figures have been challenged and, in most cases, flat out ridiculed, for using their war record for political gains. The former Secretary of State in the Obama Administration and former Senator, John F. Kerry, was challenged publically during his bid for the presidency in 2004. A group known as the Vietnam veterans for truth (also known as the Swift Boat Veterans for Truth or SBVT) questioned Mr. Kerry's military record.[7]

Although this group was later discredited, their impact during the election was undeniable. [8] The Vietnam Conflict stands as the ultimate *"Litmus test"* for most politicians seeking to establish their foreign policy credentials. But Vietnam still lingers as an unresolved issue in Indochina. It symbolizes the unfinished American engagement in the region. Many American presidents have had a say in the conflict even after it ended.

RESTORING RELATIONS WITH VIETNAM

Since the end of the war, American leaders, including Ronald Reagan, George H. W. Bush, and Bill Clinton, have sought closure in Vietnam. For the most part, these efforts have been in futility. The reason is that Cambodia was still a major prize the American government was not willing to give up. The American government demanded that any possibility to restore diplomatic relations with the Vietnamese government must begin with the Communist regime's pulling out all of its troops from Cambodia.

In the early 1990s, several attempts had been made under the guise of President George H. W. Bush (of course) to restore relations with Vietnam. On April 1991, the Bush administration reached out to the Vietnamese regime. Since that time, the relations between the United States and Vietnam had slowly, but steadily, been restored.[9]

In 1995, President Bill Clinton sought to restore diplomatic relations with Vietnam for good.[10] But the understanding is that the Vietnamese government wanted those relations as well, though they did not actively seek the United States' sincere friendship. The American government had imposed a crippling economic embargo on the Communist regime. It could also be said that the Vietnamese government also sought to ease the diplomatic tension between the two nations. In the end, these efforts paid off for the United States.

Critics were reluctant to give credits to President Clinton for restoring diplomatic ties with Vietnam. They often pointed out, satirically I might add, "President Clinton, someone who avoided serving in the war, had closed this bitter chapter in American history.[11] Nonetheless, it could be said that since 1995, the relations between the United States and Vietnam had officially been restored.

Twenty years later, on July 2, 2015, President Bill Clinton visited Vietnam. Without a doubt, this visit occurred within the realm of solidifying American relations with the Vietnamese state. But of course, it was most likely a way of commemorating the effects of the decades-old conflict. It is also worthy of mention that President Clinton's visit ostensibly took place in the context of marking the 20th anniversary of his own initiative to reinstate diplomatic relations with the Communist regime.[12]

During his visit, former President Bill Clinton stated that he was proud to have resumed relations with America's former foe in Southeast Asia twenty years ago. He echoed that the normalization of relations with Vietnam is among the highlights of his presidency.[13]

During his July 2 speech, former President Clinton echoed that, it is important for the two nations to "Heal the wounds of war and guild bonds of genuine friendship and to provide proof in an increasingly divided world that cooperation was far better than conflict."[14] Since the Clinton era, other American presidents have tried to improve diplomatic relationships with the Vietnamese regime. Recently, President Barack Obama signed a proclamation, which he dedicated to commemorating the 50th anniversary of the war.[15]

THE POLITICS OF WAR

MANUFACTURING THE VIETNAM WAR

CHAPTER NINE

9. POLITICAL SUPPORT FOR VIETNAM

THE VIETNAM HOSTILITIES had some lasting effects on American society as well. As previously articulated, the war helped sharpened citizen scrutiny regarding the American involvement in foreign conflicts. The war also had a huge impact on the debate regarding why, when, and how the American government should send military personnel in supranational situations.

As I pointed out in the anterior segment, before Vietnam, this was a completely different reality. But at some point, the American people conspicuously sought to take control of their country's foreign policy initiatives. Of course, not everyone agreed back then as to the right course of action in Vietnam. As Rudy DeLeon points out, Americans debated *"vigorously"* and in a polarizing manner as to "How to end the war in Vietnam."[1]

Nonetheless, the understanding is that things have changed since then. Presently, there is a bit of unity in America, particularly when it comes to committing U.S. troops to international conflicts. Views seldom diverge when it comes to committing American troop abroad, notably if there is the slight chance that other countries or foreign entities (i.e., NATO or the United Nations) could provide the necessary military supports in order to resolve the issue. For the most part, the American people do not want to commit U.S. troops in unnecessary global conflicts.

Other long-term effects from the Vietnam War are worth mentioning here as well, including the psychological repercussions from the fighting.[2] The ramifications of this military scuffle still linger in American foreign policy initiatives. From an historical standpoint, there is a tendency to lambast American foreign policy. That is to say, because of Vietnam, most people are afraid to trust their government in matters pertaining to wars.

THE MILITARY INDUSTRIAL COMPLEX

There is the understanding that many people in Washington are warmongers. The pervading belief is that the United States is under the emprise of what is commonly referred to as the *"Military-Industrial Complex,"* which feeds on wars.[3] The presumption here is that there are those who are determined to find any means to go to war, no matter what the consequences of such wars are or no matter what these consequences could be.

The supposition here is that Vietnam was the result of politicians who wanted to commit America to wars without considering the consequences of these conflicts. Most people were highly critical of U.S. foreign policy during Vietnam.[4] This was also the core of popular anger against the war itself. Reasoning from this fact, the presumption is that Vietnam was not America's war.

The view is that some people wanted the Vietnam War at all costs. In other words, they did not really care for its long-term consequences. But ascertaining the extent to which these views are genuine is not the subject of this text. That being said, I am of the opinion that such apprehensions could be discerned through the halls of history.

It must be noted that the recent American involvement in Afghanistan and Iraq seems to give a bit of credence to the notion that some people would do anything to go to war no matter the consequences of such actions.[5] Indeed, either Afghanistan or Iraq could have turned into another Vietnam. Some might even say that Iraq was very close to turning into another nightmare for the American military, which appeared very similar to certain aspects of the Vietnam Conflict itself.

It did not seem like American officials, including civilian and military leaders, had learned much from their errors during Vietnam. To that degree, some observers often see little or no difference between these conflicts and Vietnam.[6] Of course, the extent to which those who hold such a view are on the right side of history could be the subject of debate.[7]

Despite views to the contrary, there is no doubt that the Vietnam War altered American politics (i.e., internationally and domestically) in ways unimaginable. On both sides of the political spectrum, people held different views about the war. Democrats tended to be against it, while Republicans tended to prop it up. In the end, however, both Democrats and Republicans acted in tandem to end the war.

Was there a true political divide against the Vietnam War? The answer could easily be in the negative. However, to this day, an objective answer eludes most inquirers.

As I sought to demonstrate in the previous segment, Vietnam was not always a bad war. There was a bit of a political unity to get involved in the conflict. Calculatingly, at least in the beginning of the war itself, both Democrats and Republicans provided strong supports to war efforts. My understanding is that the decision to get involved (militarily of course) in Vietnam was initially a bi-partisan endeavor.[8]

In the event that there were any political divide back then, one could say that they might be understood as relatively inconsequential, at least during the early stages of the war. But towards the end of the conflict, politics outwardly played a more prominent role in ending the American involvement in Southeast Asia. For these reasons, we should not overlook the impact of domestic issues on the withdrawal decision itself.

THE GULF OF TONKIN

On August 4, 1964, the United States Congress passed a joint resolution (also known as the Gulf of Tonkin Resolution), which gave President Lyndon Johnson the authority to increase the United States involvement in the war between North and South Vietnam.[9] This piece of legislation provided the legal foundation for the American military presence in the region. In subsequent years, Democrat and Republican administrations seemed committed to victory in Vietnam.

It must also be noted that, at least initially, there were few dissenting voices against the war. But that does not mean that there were not those who had a different viewpoint regarding the necessity for the conflict. Still, it is worth pointing out that those who opposed any escalation of the conflict and voiced their staunch disapproval for the Tonkin Resolution, for instance, had been politically chastised or even marginalized.[10] There were no incentives to voice displeasure against Vietnam.

The war was clearly the result of a political consensus to impose a version of American idealism in Southeast Asia. Because of the popularity of the worldview that led to the conflict itself, no one was willing to refute the war. The common understanding was that refuting the war was akin to refuting America's stance in the world. At least, this was the sentiment espoused by most observers, notably during the early stages of the conflict.

A Broad Mandate

The Tonkin resolution was considered a vague piece of legislature, which engaged the Americans in Vietnam with little mandates or no clearly set limitations. Many observers viewed the American intervention in Indochina as a pretext to instill a larger dominion in the region. The resolution to go to war with North Vietnam had two purposes.

On the one hand, the resolution afforded President Johnson the authority to take the necessary measure to retaliate against the Communist regime (i.e., North Vietnam). [11] On the other hand, it also gave the American government broad latitude in the region. Overall, the resolution gave the American government the capacity or the authority to promote the maintenance of planetary peace and security in Southeast Asia. [12] Subsequently, both Presidents Lyndon Johnson and Richard Nixon used the document to justify a broader military presence in Indochina.

My point is that it could not be said that Vietnam was the war of one party, as opposed to the entire nation. Although the war was not inspired by ordinary Americans, it was apparently embraced, at least initially by both major political parties (i.e., Democrats and Republicans). This was a war fought at the deepest level of the American government. Ironically, what, as a sequel, ended the conflict could also be discerned as a deep political divide in American society at the time.

Democrats are known to take positions against wars, even when they instigated many of them in the past. Nevertheless, the extent to which a political division led to the end of the conflict is not well understood. Within that context, it is important to evaluate the role of politics or political ideologies in facilitating the fermentation of the Vietnam War.

CHAPTER TEN

10. POPULAR WRITINGS ABOUT VIETNAM

THE LITERATURE IS FILLED with literary works and other types of writings about Vietnam. Some authors have written about the reasons the war was fought, while others tend to focus on the consequences of the conflict itself. From my vantage point, most works are inadequate. Many compilations about the Vietnam War (for instance, non-scholarly works) are short stories. They conventionally relate already known facts about the events that took place in the region.

In spite of the aforementioned shortcomings, I must acknowledge that most works about Vietnam are very informative. Bearing in mind, I do not seek to minimize the informational value of these works. But in the present work, I propose a different approach regarding the reason the war ended. Although my arguments are not novel per se, they project a different perspective in the debate.

While there is no dearth of information about the war, few written works are academically oriented. In this regard, it is equally important to talk about the conflict analytically. Thus, it is important to discuss the nature of the Vietnam War from an academic standpoint.

It is not evident that there was a real distension among the political establishment against the war. It must also be noted that the public was increasingly anti-war. Nonetheless, local politicians seemed to operate under a different set of motives either to support the war or to disapprove it.

I would reiterate that, at least in the beginning, there was a political unification for the war. But as the public became disenchanted with the American involvement in the region, politics became a convenient tool to end the war. With this in view, Vietnam could be best understood through the lenses of politics or political ideology as well.

APPROACHES TO THE CONFLICT

The Vietnam Conflict could be assessed from various angles. But there are few instances where one could be neutral about this subject. To that extent, it would be naïve to seek neutrality in any attempt to understand the war. To restate a previous assertion, there is no consensus about the war and its effects.

To this day, an official winner has never been declared. Thus, any attempt to elucidate what transpired during the war could be slanted or could be laden with biases. By far, this book is not the exception to that reality.

What I am saying here is that assessing the nature of the Vietnam War in all objectivity could be a complex undertaken. Still, this is not necessarily a difficult subject to decipher. But one caveat worth pointing out is the structure or the organization of the book itself. Thus, the reason I do not claim any authority on the subject.

The arguments featured here center on the notion that the United States had been forced out of Vietnam. That is to say, the Americans could no longer sustain a military presence in Indochina. But the main point I seek to legislate is that America was not forced out of the region by external forces or forces within Vietnam per se. There were other issues at play. Domestic issues in particular on the face of it put a dent in war efforts, which, in the course of time, led to the end of the conflict.

Another contention is that the war ended because of America's own governmental actions. Here, I am referring to America's own policy-making mechanism. There is no doubt that internal issues had an impact in the way the problem was approached. Such issues, in the eleventh hour, seemingly dictated the policy direction of the country.

At some point, policy makers had no choice. They had to yield to the *vox populi* (the voice of the people or « La voix du people » as it were) or the opinions of the majority. To that extent, it is worth pointing out that the American people played a significant role in ending the conflict.

At this point in the debate, it seems relevant to echo that domestic issues constituted an important factor in winding down the American involvement in Indochina. Inescapably, there were those who wanted the country to maintain the course. But those who wanted an immediate withdrawal from the region appeared to convey that understanding louder than the other camp did. Thus, it is important to take this aspect of the conflict into account as well as we go alone.

A Media War

The Vietnam War was among the first major conflicts where members of the press had a considerable amount of access to the day-to-day activities of the American military. Vietnam was also the first conflict where the media enjoyed full freedom to the press, which gave journalists the ability to report the war as they saw it unfolded.[1] But for most observers, the media's role in exposing what was taking place in Vietnam incited unnecessary contentions, which also led to political backlashes against both the government and the conduct of the war itself.

The position held by both pro and anti war observers centered on the notion that the media played a significant role in captivating public interest about the war. But the consequences of this broad media libertinage also led to an unnecessary public scrutiny of military clashes in the jungle of Cambodia.

The common belief is that the media weakened the administration's efforts to win the war. The media also precipitated the anti-war movement on U.S. soils, they said. The contention is that images that paraded on television screens across the nation had a negative impact on the consciousness of the American public.

In contrast to the previous argument, some commentators have argued that the media was a powerful force during the jungle battles. They informed the public about the reality of the war. But other observers have also argued that the media played a detrimental role in the war. To that extent, understandings about the role of the media during the Vietnam Conflict could be described as bitterly divisive.[2]

It is true that the Vietnam War was heavily documented. Even so, very little is known about the day-to-day operations of the conflict itself. As a matter of common practice, the nature of war efforts is not necessarily revealed to the public. Vietnam was not the exception to this common practice.

From a policy standpoint, the war is a mystery to most. What truly transpired in Vietnam during the fighting is not always depicted accurately. We do not know the full extent of the nature of the conduct of the war.

Of course, we know that the President of the United States was a major player in the decision-making. We could also agree that Congress played a big role in the conflict. But other than a few known political figures that we know for a fact were involved in the decision-making mechanism, it is not clear who had the ultimate power to influence the final decision.

To reiterate a previous assertion, Vietnam was undoubtedly a complicated conflict. It was so both politically and militarily. Still, I do not seek to rewrite the history of Vietnam here. While taking into account the contentious nature of the conflict, I only hope to shed some lights on the events, not to create more controversies through the arguments proposed herein.

It is worthy of note that the apparent rift against the media was mostly punctuated along ideological lines. Liberals and conservatives had different opinions regarding the credibility of politicians based on the accounts painted by the media. But it was obvious that a clear divide existed between the media and the government during Vietnam. Daniel Hallin, for instance, notes, "it is widely accepted across the political spectrum that the relation between the media and the government during Vietnam was in fact one of conflict."[3]

REFUTING CRITICISMS AGAINST THE MEDIA

For most commentators, there were people who would purposefully misrepresent the facts of the Vietnam War. Unless one has had a direct experience in Vietnam, relating information about the conflict should be done with caution, some have argued. Still, one could hardly refute the notion that the media had been an influential tool, which eventually shaped the political outcome of the war.

I understand that some observers might question the extent of the role the media played in facilitating the end of the conflict. But it could be argued that the role the media played was vital. The media clearly provided the framework for the public to assess the necessity for the conflict. Seeing the devastation from the battlefield had a big impact on the way people reacted to Vietnam and the U.S. involvement in the region. Thus, it would not be farfetched to claim that the media catapulted or perhaps precipitated the end of the war.

I am not sure whether anyone could refute the validity of the above apprehension. We know that the war was televised. Not the worse, the American activities in the region were frequently commented in local newspapers. To that degree, it must be acknowledge that the media played an undeniable role in the conflict.

I am positive that most people would agree that the media was quintessential in depicting a side of the war that the American government would have never disclosed to the public. But the argument could be made that the media influenced the political discourse about Vietnam in many ways. It also affected the social discourse by providing a reference point to anti-war activists.

I must point out that it was not easy criticizing the war. Most observers often evoke patriotism when they speak about the Vietnam War. Some people have a romantic view regarding what truly transpired in the jungle of Laos and Cambodia. Of course, it is not their fault. There was a deliberate attempt to undo criticisms against the war (*See* Chapter 3/The Cover Up).

Popular culture, for instance, has immortalized the Vietnam War (or aspects of it) in many respects.[4] In an attempt to provide a more positive picture of the war, there was a tendency to *"Showcase"* Vietnam as the place where the American military had to fight evil in its hut. Many people tend to present a side of the war that might not be accurate. Here, however, I will not dwell on this issue. Nevertheless, it is worth pointing out these important aspects of the war, while we try to wrap our heads around what truly transpired in Indochina almost half a century ago.

From an academic viewpoint, fewer writings about the war could help refute doubts about the role the United States played in the conflict. When it comes to the sheer level of brutality that was displayed during the war, views extensively diverge. Nonetheless, it was evident that there were horrible actions on both sides.

The Vietnam War occurred so many years ago that even the people who fought in the conflict, one can assume, do not remember the reason they were part of it. Not but what, few people could catalogue themselves as an authority on the subject. But it is still plausible to decipher Vietnam from the lens of those who truly experienced it.

Let me point out that the positions outlined throughout this document thus far do not reflect unadulterated opinions. Rather, they are a compilation of ideas, which are often echoed in the literature. They include views expressed by Vietnam veterans, historians, and scholars (*See* the Bibliography section to learn more).

CHAPTER ELEVEN

11. LEAVING VIETNAM

BETWEEN MARCH AND APRIL 1975, the United States military evacuated a number of strategic points throughout the Vietnam region. But the most famous evacuation was the one that took place in the city of Saigon itself. This particular rescue mission caught the world's attention, when hundreds, if not thousands of Vietnamese dissidents, could be seen stranded on the rooftop of an American embassy. They had been awaiting marine helicopters to airlift them out of the city.

Some of the images captured about this event were very telling. They depicted a desperate situation where many people were willing to climb up walls adjacent to the building that lodged the American Embassy, at the peril of their own lives, in order to leave the city or perhaps the country. This particular moment is often referred to as the *"Fall of Saigon."*

Immediately after the American troops departed from the region, North Vietnamese forces took control of the city. At the end of the day, the Northern regime also took control over the whole country. The downfall of the city itself (i.e., Saigon) culminated with the end of the conflict itself. What could explain the reason [or reasons] the Americans withdrew from the region at this particular juncture?

Various scenarios have been proposed in order to explain the reason for the withdrawal. But most explanations could be categorized as pure speculations. Few people have a sense of what truly transpired at the American governmental level. Few outsiders understood the policy reasons that led to the evacuation itself. But few observers could relate to the average inquirer the rationale for the decision to withdraw from Indochina.

I could say with an utmost confidence that the reason America exited the region is not clear. Observers usually have different positions regarding when and why the Americans left Vietnam. Still, the pervading belief is that the exit was timed and calculated. But most of the people who experienced the war either personally or vicariously often hold conflicting views regarding the events that took place in both the jungle of Vietnam and at home (i.e., in Washington).

No doubt, Vietnam was a very difficult period in American history. The war affected American society in various aspects. But even those who did not experience the war directly tend to view its conduct from distinct lenses. I recognize that, while some observers might agree that the American military was forced to leave the region, others might reject that view.

Nonetheless, it could not be argued that the war ended cordially. No formal acknowledgement was entered between the parties involved, which would indicate that the conflict had ended. To reiterate a previous observation, the United States was no longer part of the war since 1973, at least officially.

AN UNYIELDING COMMITMENT

The American government's support to the South Vietnamese regime indicated they were also committed to the region. All indications suggested that they wanted a victory; they were deeply entrenched in war efforts. The American government seemed to have an unyielding obligation to help the regime in the South defeat North Vietnamese forces.

From a political perspective, there could not be a tie in Vietnam. Either the American military or the North Vietnamese army had to be defeated before the war could end. But from a military standpoint, this argument could be hard to make. The longer the war lasted, the more political support for war efforts eroded.

From a strategic angle, however, there was a reality on the battlefield. That is to say, neither the Americans nor the Vietcong forces could claim a military victory in Vietnam. In the process of conducting the war, both sides sustained heavy damages. Surely, there were instances where the military might of the United States was evident. But it must also be said that there were instances where the cunning of the Vietcong army was astonishingly en exergue.

The month of April marked a turning point in the conflict. Congress rejected President Ford's request. The American government could no longer help the South Vietnamese regime maintain a military edge over North Vietnamese forces. As a result, the end of the war appeared imminent.

It must be noted that Congress did not formally deny all forms of funding initiatives for South Vietnam. While the legislative body did not approve some form of funding, it did approve other types of aids. For example, Congress approved humanitarian aids for Vietnam.

What I am saying here is that it is unequivocal that Congress did not approve the funding for military assistance. Nevertheless, the legislative branch did approve funding for military evacuation throughout the region. That being said, it must also be noted that the amount of funding Congress approved for Vietnam was not sufficient in order to help the South Vietnamese regime win the war.

APPROVING THE MILITARY EVACUATION

On April 21, 1975, the House Appropriations Committee voted 36 to 15 to approve $165 million in humanitarian aid to South Vietnam.[1] Despite the fact that there was staunch opposition in Congress to provide financial aid and other types of support to South Vietnam, "The requests for humanitarian assistance and permission to use force in evacuating Americans received a more favorable treatment."[2] Certainly, there were concerns that using combat troops to evacuate American personnel, South Vietnamese allies, and other supporters, could lead to more hostility in the region.

Some observers feared that this move could lead to more casualties, specifically on the American side. There was also a sense of inquietude that such a move could lead to the imprisonment of members of the American forces.[3] Thus, there was a reluctance to evacuate the region in haste.

Despite that cautious approach to exiting the region, the Americans left Vietnam in an unprecedented alacrity. It is unequivocal that the end of the

Vietnam Conflict was very chaotic. The month of April in particular was extremely active; it was a decisive moment in the war.

During that month, the American government initiated several military activities, which were aimed at evacuating embassy personnel from the region. The military was on high alert. Their mission consisted of airlifting embassy personnel stranded in various parts of Vietnam.

There was not a uniformed approach regarding the best way to exit Vietnam. There was no consensus about war exiting initiatives. As a result, many observers tend to look at the military actions to evacuate American personnel from different prisms.

While some observers commonly refer to these events as evacuations, others tend to view them as a turning point in the conflict. For some commentators, these moments engendered the end of the war. Others have argued that the last hours of the conflict defined the American government's incapacity to conquer Indochina. I would submit that there is some truth to the above viewpoints.

While views habitually diverge on the nature of the war itself, what is certain is that this military conflict brought a lot of pain and suffering to a number of families. Those that lost loved ones during battles or outside of hostilities (including military personnel and civilians) were even more disconcerted about the outcomes. Some observers even called the Vietnam debacle a *"senseless"* war.

The viewpoints often echoed in the halls of history is that Vietnam was the first war the Americans lost in a long time. Although some pundits might refute that argument, there is enough evidence to suggest that America did not win the war. Even as a child, I remember hearing people around me saying that the Americans got *"A beaten in Vietnam."*

From a different angle, there was the understanding that the Americans gave Vietnamese fighters a run for their money (so to speak). Popular Hollywood movies reinforced that belief in many ways. In those movies, American heroism and American military bravura were very much in exergue. A *"Kick-ass"* attitude from the American military is often projected in popular Hollywood movies. Vietnamese fighters, on the other hand, are generally portrayed as ruthless villains, whom deserve no pity or mercy.

The reality is that the war was a lost cause; at least on the American side. At some point, American leaders had fewer options, but to leave. Still, the understanding is that the Americans decided to leave Vietnam when they felt that it was necessary to do so.

Here, I do not refute the previous argument per se. But it must also be noted that most people believed that anti-war protests at home weakened American position in Indochina. From that angle, the argument is that these protests, in the end, had an effect on war efforts both at home and abroad.

AN IMMORAL WAR

There was also the sense that the Vietnam War was wide of the American foreign policy mark. It was a mistaken military venture. It was an immoral war to say the least. Some refused to take part in it. Famous entertainers and politicians did everything to avoid serving in Vietnam. Muhammad Ali, a popular athlete (boxer) at the time refused to take part in the war.[4]

No question about it; Vietnam was a mess. Politicians could no longer galvanize the necessary support at home for the troops. I would contend that there is some truth to that argument as well.

This view also suggested that the United States could have won the war militarily. But most observers would agree that the war was a military blunder. American fighters were ill equipped and insufficiently trained to fight in the jungle of Vietnam. This was a guerrilla war and America had little or no chance to crush the North Vietnamese fighters on their home turf.

For other observers, America left the region after winning the war. But it is not clear whether one could provide any tangible proofs to support such a view. From a different angle, many people seemed convinced that America did not leave Vietnam on its own. Hence, the reason the Americans were pushed out of the region. Evidently, this is the point I sought to echo in this text.

It could be reasonably deduced that the advancements of North Vietnamese fighters were irreversible. On the face of the Northern military progress, South Vietnamese fighters had fewer options. The ultimate capture of Saigon appeared imminent. The humiliation could have been worst, in the event that the North Vietnamese fighters were able to capture the American Embassy along with a few American officials inside of it. Perhaps in an attempt to avoid such a prospect, the Americans realized that they had no viable options; they had to leave Vietnam immediately.

It would be difficult, if not almost impossible, to refute the above presumption, considering the reality on the ground at the time. No doubt, it was a lost war in Vietnam. But for some observers, the Americans simply did not want to admit defeat. I tend to espouse a similar view.

WINNING BY LOSING

The momentum gained by the Viet Cong fighters seemed unstoppable. To illustrate this assertion, some observers often point out the amount of casualties sustained by the American military. They also tend to point out the chaotic evacuation from Saigon, right before the Communist takeover of the country. There is some undeniable truth to that view.[5]

Another rationale about the evacuation is often echoed in the literature. This understanding is worthy of our examination here as well, albeit summarily. From this angle, the belief is that the American government had chosen a different strategy in order to win the conflict.

Since the Americans could no longer sustain a military presence in Indochina, they had espoused a different avenue in order to cripple the Communist regime. The argument is that the American government would withdraw from Vietnam militarily. But on a different theater, they would engage the Vietnamese regime more efficiently. The belief is that, instead of engaging in military clashes, the Americans would impose harsh economic sanctions onto the North Vietnamese regime.

In my opinion, this is an absurdist slant to deciphering the Vietnam War itself. Nevertheless, many people truly believe that America had all the winning cards all along. But the extent to which this is an accurate picture of the conflict is not always obvious.

A few things are clear about the war. First, America was not winning when it left the region. Second, by the spring of 1975, the South Vietnamese government was also on its last leg. Their army was in shamble. Third, the resilience of North Vietnamese fighters was incomprehensible. Hence, there was no tangible way that the Americans could have pulled off a victory from Vietnam. But this is just my own assessment of the issues.

At this point, let me say that answering the many questions posed in the introductory section succinctly could be extremely difficult. Of course, I have tried to approach some of these questions on a piece meal basis here.

But I reckon that I have not been able to offer a conclusive appraisal as to the reason the war ultimately ended.

Granted, without a conceptual framework, any approach to providing some form of an answer to the aforementioned inquiries could be impossible. Any answer could be convoluted, incoherent, and one-sided. Such answers could also be contested and refuted. Nonetheless, I am not of the opinion that the Americans won the Vietnam War.

VIETNAM AND OTHER WARS

To this day, what happened in Vietnam is still within the realm of a mystery, at least from a policy standpoint. Understandably, one could only speculate about what truly transpired during the war itself. All the same, the decision-making mechanisms of the American government at the time were not of course obvious to most observers, including to those of us that might have little or no background in policymaking (e.g., a layperson in American domestic politics and foreign policy).

It is not clear what led to the war. Certainly, we know that President Truman offered to help France against the Vietnamese peasants' uprising. However, the reason he sought to help the French is still unsettled. In other words, the true motive for the war still eludes most observers.

The strategy America used to fight its battles in Vietnam was uncertain. For most observers, it was not apparent whether the United States had a specific plan to win the war. The argument here is that it was not clear whether the Americans had a clear strategy in order to win and not just plans to engage in battles or plans to instigate devastating military bombing campaigns.

Others are convinced that the war was ill conceived since the beginning. American military forces underestimated their opponents. Some observers have even contended that there was no exit strategy in Vietnam. As unthinkable as this may sound, all indications suggest that the decision to end the conflict was unscripted or unpredicted. At best, this was a rush decision.

Perhaps Vietnam was a blip in American foreign policy. Perhaps it was a major event. But American officials never seemed to miss the opportunity to minimize their failure in the region. There are no official acknowledgments regarding the many mistakes, which American officials seemingly made in Vietnam. One could not avoid wondering whether American policymakers learned a valuable lesson from the Vietnam fiasco. The answer could definitely be in the negative.

The reality could not be more evident than it is now. Vietnam was a punitive war. Many lives were lost. There is no way around that fact.

The Americans did not get their way. Now, you could label the actions that led to the end of the conflict a strategic move. You could also refer to the war as a lost, a failure, a withdrawal, or a policy change in Indochina. But whatever you say, you could not refer to Vietnam as another American victory. You could not add Vietnam on the list of international trophies the Americans won, notably in the Asian Continent. From my understanding, the fact that the Americans left Vietnam the manner that they did could not be equated to a victory in any way, shape, or form.

The Americans lost in Vietnam. There is no way to undermine this reality. The question worth examining is why that was the case. We must also ascertain what led to the demise of American officials at this particular crossroad. But the salient question worth ascertaining is whether the Americans learned their lesson from Vietnam? Answers are not clear.

As inferred in previous chapters, subsequent wars carry some resemblance to the Vietnam Conflict itself, including the wars in both Iraq and Afghanistan. These wars could have easily become another Vietnam. Just like in the jungles of Laos and Cambodia, the extent to which the United States had a clear strategy to win its battles in the aforementioned conflicts was not obvious.

I recognize that the comparison could be minimal. In other words, there are little similarities in terms of the two countries' geography and the profile of the conflicts themselves. That is to say, Vietnam was not perforce Iraq; it was neither Afghanistan. But that does not mean there were not some astonishing similarities, particularly when it comes to the fighting styles of the insurgents in Iraq.

It could also be said that the overall reasons that instigated these conflicts were different. In consideration of the foregoing, it could be said that the policy rationale that led to the two conflicts appeared very similar. But when it comes to Vietnam in particular, it is worth noting that haphazard explanations could only invite erroneous assumptions about the actors who made the ultimate decision to withdraw from the region. I did not wish to approach the Vietnam War from such an angle here.

CHAPTER TWELVE

12. Examining War-Exit Strategies

BEFORE WE USE Allison's models in order to understand the last executive decision in the Vietnam War, it is imperative that we examine the policy reasons that instigated the conflict in the first place. It is also important to examine the policy mechanisms that facilitated its continuity. Officially, the war lasted ten years (i.e., between 1965 and 1975). But it could also be said that the conflict lasted longer than that.

A number of observers noted that the war lasted approximately two decades, if not longer. Other commentators have pointed out that the United States attempt to create an independent South Vietnamese state lasted more the two decades and a half.[1] It could be adumbrated that the American presence throughout Indochina was not a mere coincidence.

As discussed in previous segments, the initial American involvement in the region began in the mid-1940s (*See* Chapter 6). My contention is that a thorough examination of the motive for the war might allow a better assessment of the origin of the military clash itself. This might enable us to ascertain who initiated the war, who financed it, and who had the power to end it.

The war was the product of several decisions. Those decisions were taken by an amalgam of decision makers. But the most important decision makers in the conflict were the United States Congress and the executive branch.

My contention here is that Vietnam was not the doing of one individual. The foundation of this military venture in Indochina depended on a corollary of decision makers within the American government. Those that conducted the war included both civilian and military leaders.

The governmental entities that initiated and, possibly, managed the war might include several congressional committees and the United States President, including high-level cabinet members. It could also be said that decision makers had a different level of involvement in the conduct of the war. Thus, the conduct of the war had several layers.

The Vietnam War was a governmental affair at the deepest level. For example, while President Harry Truman was the first to involve the United States in the conflict, President Lyndon Johnson was the first to send combat troops in the region. On the strength of that argument, it is paramount to examine the role of both presidents in the initial decision to enter the conflict. But these are among the limitations of the present work. As should be apparent by now, I do not examine the issues from such an angle in this manuscript.

UNABLE TO MAINTAIN THE COURSE

As a means to understand the reason the United States withdrew from Vietnam, it is vital to examine the role both the Legislative and executive branches played in fermenting the conflict. At the time, American embraced a policy of containment. [2] Understandably, it seems logical that few American presidents wanted to get out of Vietnam without accomplishing their goals, which was to rid Vietnam and other surrounding countries of Communism.[3]

Since the end of World War II and the rise of the Soviet Union as a threat for world peace, U.S. military interventions overseas were usually tied to the containment of Communism. [4] The Vietnam Conflict could be examined from such an angle. It could be said that war policy decisions within the American government were inscribed within the realm of that understanding.

Another goal, as stated by President Gerald Ford himself during a speech to congressional members in 1975, included the notion that it was necessary to instill democracy throughout Indochina. President Ford reiterated that the United States had an obligation to maintain its engagement to instill individual freedom and democracy in the region.[5] But a few weeks later, in a staunch contrast, the President ordered the evacuation of Saigon.

Several aspects of the reason (or possible reasons) that led the United States to get involved in the region could also be examined based on a larger foreign policy framework. For instance, the Americans sought to insert hegemony in Southeast Asia. In that sense, one might say that America's foreign policy initiatives were outwardly geared towards preventing both the Soviet Union and China from holding a grip over the entire region.

On the other hand, it is important to examine the manner in which individual leaders packaged their messages to each other. It is also imperative to understand who had the last word in the decision-making process. But no matter how we approach the conflict itself, it must be echoed that Vietnam was not the doing of one actor or a single entity within the American government itself.

Popular animosity against the war made it almost impossible to maintain the course in Vietnam. From this vantage point, one might say that the American involvement in the Vietnam War ended because domestic supports for military actions in the region dwindled. This decrease of support occurred to a point where it was no longer politically feasible to advocate for maintaining the course in Vietnam.

The lack of support at home had a negative effect on war efforts abroad. As debated in chapter seven, there was a similar sentiment overseas. Fewer nations supported the American military pursuit in Vietnam. That is to say, as public supports for the war eroded at home, so did political supports both at home and abroad.

This situation also had a cascading effect. As political supports for the military involvement in Vietnam dwindled, so did the financial supports to sustain military activities throughout the Indochina region (*See* Figure 1). At that point, Congress became the only entity that could end the war. The Legislators held the power of the purse.[6] They surely yielded such power when they refused to approve the financial aid, which had been requested by the executive branch. This is where the role of Congress was vital in ending the Vietnam War.

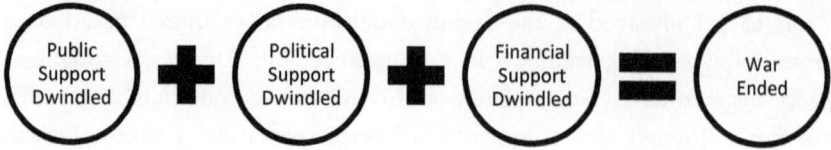

Figure 1: War Ending Sequence

THE WITHDRAWAL POLICY

After the Gulf of Tonkin incident, Congress authorized the U.S. involvement in Vietnam. Although in the beginning most members of Congress appeared fond of the war, their views of the conduct of the conflict itself were mitigated towards the end of the conflict. In early 1970s, most members of Congress wanted to end the war. As a result, policy makers were cornered, for they had little or no other means to implement their desired courses of action.[7]

American policy makers were forced to make policy choices that were evidently incompatible with their wishes. They ended the war prematurely. The embassy evacuation was unmistakably the last important decision in the war. However, that decision was perhaps based on a larger policy framework. Hence, it is important to examine such a policy in order to get a sense of what truly transpired in Vietnam.

All indications suggest that the American government ran out of money. But this understanding also suggests that the country was in a dire financial situation. Of course, we know that this was not necessarily the case. At the time, America was not going through a tough time, at least not financially.

The question we must ascertain is to what extent insufficient funds was the reason the war ended. I am not sure. I did not find a piece of literature, which suggests that America's finances had dwindled to a point where the

American government could no longer finance the war. What we know is that there was a reluctance to keep funding the war. That reluctance was outwardly motivated by a collar of reasons, including domestic pressure to end the conflict.

President Gerald Ford wanted additional funding for Vietnam. The United States had also promised the Vietnamese government unconditional financial supports. The problem is that none of this was possible anymore. Congress had put a roadblock to the American government's initiatives in the region.

At some point, the executive branch became cognizant of its incapability to accomplish its goals in Indochina. The reality on the ground was also clear. The military could not eradicate the threat posed by North Vietnamese forces. Even the stability of the South Vietnamese regime was put in question. Thus, the viability of the southern regime was very precarious towards the end of the war.

The United States withdrew from the region in 1975, in disgrace I might add. Still, this view might be refuted, depending on whom you ask. But is that the entire story of the war? Was there something brewing behind the walls of Congress or inside the oval office (i.e., in the White House), which was not apparent to most observers. How to best approach the policy rationale that led to the end of the conflict itself? The next few chapters will attempt to shed some lights on these questions.

NO OTHER ALTERNATIVES

It could not be said that America left Vietnam on its own. Few people could argue that America had not lost control of Indochina before it withdrew from the region. As Robert Stalnaker suggested, the war was a mess.[8] The Americans could no longer handle themselves in the conflict. To reaffirm a previously stated viewpoint, leaving Vietnam was the only viable option for the American government at the time,

To restate, the present volume could not answer all the questions posed in anterior chapters based on serendipitous analyses of the conflict. But with a bit of certainty, I would say that many of these questions could be answered based on the discussions echoed in previous sections. We could also infer these answers based on the facts recounted in the literature. But there is more to the issues. We need to examine the withdrawal decision closer.

What I am trying to say here is that I could not answer many of the questions posed here objectively. I must also point out that the approach I have espoused in this text is geared towards neutrality. But I understand that such neutrality might be hard to have.

The goal is to examine the policy reasons that led to the end of the Vietnam War as cogently as possible. But I understand that this is a daunting task. The extent to which the views proffered here might make a difference in the literature could be negligible. Nonetheless, this is the only way we could ascertain, albeit to some degree, what led the Americans to depart from Vietnam in the manner that they did.

EXAMINING THE TERM "FORCE"

My position is that the Americans got out of Vietnam because they were forced to leave the region at that fastidious juncture in the conflict. But what was is it that precipitated the forced exit? For the most part, the answer is not clear.

Another assertion is that the forced exit could be examined based on the actions posed by an array of actors, including North Vietnamese fighters, the President of the United States, the American Legislature, the Media, the political climate in Washington, and the American public at large. Evidently, there is a point at which one actor's actions instigated a chain of reactions, which incited the other actors to take the position that they took in due course.

Regardless, it could not be said that the end of the war was the doing of one particular entity. These actors, on their own of course, could not force the Americans to leave Vietnam in the manner that they did. It would be shortsighted or perhaps intransigent to blame one particular entity for the forced American exit from Indochina.

By the spring of 1975, American officials [i.e., policy makers] had no other alternatives, but to leave the region. The next logical question is why these officials felt that it was necessary to leave Vietnam the moment that they did or even the disorderly fashion that they did. I will ascertain this question a bit further in the remaining parts of the text.

We must determine the meaning of the term *"forced"* in this instance. But we must do so within the context of the many questions, which have been reverberated in this document. We must explore the degree to which the American military was forced to leave Vietnam. In other words, we must acknowledge that the American military did not have other alternatives, but to leave the region.

By April 1975, most of the American troops had dwindled considerably in the region. At the time, there was no way that the American army could have been able to mount an offensive against the rise of North Vietnamese fighters. There was no immediate military solution in Vietnam.

Another question worth ascertaining is whether the decision to leave the region was based on the military deterioration of the war itself (on the American side) or whether it was based on the political decay in Washington. I am inclined to say that the political corrosion at home was at the core of the decision to withdraw from Vietnam. I will elaborate further about this point in the next few chapters.

We must make sense of the atmosphere that led to the end of the conflict. We must decipher, as accurately as feasible, who [or what] could have forced the powerful American military to leave a country like Vietnam. Since answers are not clear, we could infer that the conditions were no longer propitious for an American presence in Indochina.

But based on what I have pointed out thus far, it could be said that there is more to the withdrawal decision. Of course, I hope to offer further clarifications about the issues. We need to ascertain the matter a bit deeper. I will attempt to do just that in subsequent chapters.

FORCING AMERICA OUT

To recap, the present examination of the issues is not a revision of the history of the conflict. This text does not seek to rewrite the events that occurred in Vietnam many years ago. It is undeniable that the war was an extremely polarized event in American history. But this text is not extensive enough to reconcile all diverging viewpoints.

During the 1960s and even in the beginning of the 1970s, people held different beliefs as to the role America should play in Indochina. The war was undoubtedly the result of deeply seated American beliefs about the world. Such a worldview could not be undermined at the time. Perhaps to this day, nothing has changed. In that spirit, I am not sure that the arguments presented here thus far could change the position of those who continue to hold such a view of the world.

On the other side of the debate, some might say that American foreign policy initiatives are still based on such understanding. I did not aim at refuting that viewpoint in this text. Notwithstanding what I have just said, it is still important to explore the extent of these foreign policy approaches. Let us do so with more interest.

The previous assessments suggest that there is no doubt that the United States was forced out of Vietnam. The conditions were not propitious for them to remain in Indochina. From a military standpoint, America was losing the war. From a financial standpoint, Congress had taken a firm stance and did not seem willing to budge from its posture.

All the same, there were little or no tangible supports at home to maintain the course in Vietnam. Most Americans were fed up about the war. They wanted an immediate withdrawal from the region. As a result, the political pressure was mounting. To that degree, local politicians could not ignore their constituency on the matter of Vietnam.

From a domestic standpoint, America could no longer justify a presence in Vietnam. Of course, American politicians wanted to find a means to maintain the course at all costs. They sought to fight the war by proxy. They viewed the South Vietnamese regime as their surrogate army in the region. But these demarches failed. Congress unanimously refuted that approach. Thus, there is only one sensible alternative. That is, the Americans had to leave; they could no longer stay in Vietnam. Hence, the Americans had been forced to leave Vietnam despite their desire to stay the course.

Let us switch gear. But in order to avoid redundancy in our arguments, let us espouse a scientific approach instead. Let us rely on the intellectual tool proposed by Graham T. Allison to make sense of Vietnam and the decision that ended the conflict itself.

The Withdrawal Decision

The Allison Approach

CHAPTER THIRTEEN

13. A SCIENTIFIC APPROACH

FOR A VERY LONG TIME, historians have been debating the possible reasons the United States withdrew from Vietnam. Arguably, this was a decision, which effectively ended the Vietnam fiasco itself. But that decision also led to a number of speculations. To this day, there are many disagreements as to the origin of the policy itself.

What is certain is that the decision to withdraw from the region incited the notion that the Americans chickened out of the war because they had sustained heavy casualties. The presumption is that the Americans withdrew from Vietnam because they were on the verge of losing the war. Of course, most observers have refuted the veracity of that understanding.

On the other hand, some commentators are more pragmatic. The understanding in that camp is that Vietnam is among the few instances where the American government suffered a stunning defeat in a military conflict. For sure, there were other wars, which the American military did not fare well. But the losses in Vietnam were innumerable.

The Vietnam War left a scar in the minds of many young men and women, notably the ones who fought in the jungles of Laos and Cambodia. The war also affected those who protested against it. But only those who fought in the treacherous jungles of Vietnam truly experienced the long-term effects of the war. For these people, Vietnam was not a laughing matter. In many instances, it was a life or death situation.

As we have debated in previous segments, the Vietnam Conflict had been ongoing for many years, when Congress decided to stop funding the South Vietnamese government. By that time, the war was very unpopular. The graphic images that had been played out on television screens across the country clearly helped cast doubts about the role American troops should play in the conflict. Witnessing the level of death and destructions that the war had engendered was possibly one of the reasons public sentiments went sour.

By the mid-1960s, the sheer number of American casualties made Vietnam one of the most polarized foreign policy ventures in American history. It is worth reiterating that most Americans had a visceral reaction to the war itself. On the streets, there was a sense that, with [or without] a victory, America needed to withdraw from the region. For the most part, this position was non-negotiable and it was vigorously echoed everywhere in America.

The unpopularity of the war reached a point of no return. By that time, there was little or nothing the American government could do to convinced recalcitrant anti-war activists that staying the course in Indochina was in the country's best interests. As expected, during this juncture, anti-war movements also reached a very high level of hostility.

The country was on the verge of civil unrest. Public dissents turned into public chaos. Social unrest, in turn, led to wide spread instability. For some observers, America was on the brink of a civil war.[1]

Between the late 1960s and early 1970s (at the domestic level of course), the war had become a major symbol of youth resistance. Many activists had called upon young men and women to take a stand against the war. By that time, anti-Vietnam sentiments had grown exponentially. Calls to end the conflict had attracted "Members from college campuses, middle-class suburbs, labor unions, and governmental institutions" across the country.[2]

Anti-war protests were very popular. The movement itself "Peaked in 1968 and remained powerful throughout the duration of the conflict."[3] Such movements got more traction on university campuses across the country. By the time major combat operations officially ended in 1973, there were many casualties on both sides.[4]

The war extended through many presidencies, including John F. Kennedy, Richard Nixon, and Gerald R. Ford.[5] Over the years, political supports for the war dwindled, as the American government sought to implement [or to come up, depending on whom you ask] a winning strategy. But the American Legislature, traditionally a less influential player in foreign policy, found it increasingly difficult to support the war.[6] As a result, the influence of the legislative branch increased exponentially. Without omission, many members of Congress oppose the funding of the war.

THE MILITARY STRUGGLE

It is irrefutable that Vietnam was a tough war for the American military. But regardless of the obstacles that they faced, American officials strived to maintain their commitment to war efforts in Indochina. Between 1950 and 1975, the war had become a major political concern.[7]

Although the war took place thousands of miles away, it had a profound impact on American domestic politics.[8] Political concerns also informed the policy choices of the government. However, one particular foreign policy is the subject of this short inquiry. The focus is on the policy rationale that led to the adoption of the withdrawal decision from Vietnam.

It is important to understand the policy decision that led to the end of the war itself. The question we should be asking here is what motivated politicians and policy makers to adopt a different stance in Vietnam. As I have sought to demonstrate throughout this manuscript, the American government did not withdraw voluntarily from the region.

The war was not going well. But there was a deliberate attempt to change the narrative. Proponents of the war sought to convey the understanding that some people wanted to sabotage war efforts. The supposition here is that victory was within sights.

Nonetheless, the reality on the ground painted a different picture about the conflict, which could not be undermined with propaganda alone. For opponents of the war, Congress had to act. Indeed, Congress did act. But the manner in which Congress acted is often regarded as a flagrant disregard for the separation of the branches of government, namely the Legislative and the Executive.

This view is based on an illogical argument. We know for certainty that Congress ended the war by yielding its constitutional powers. In addition,

Congress used the so-called "Power of the purse" to halt the American military role in Vietnam. Few could claim that this act was unconstitutional.

When the war became untenable, President Gerald Ford ordered the evacuation of the remaining American personnel in Vietnam. No doubt, the evacuation was hasty and, by any estimations, chaotic. Many people left in Marine helicopters, from the rooftop of an American embassy in Saigon. That month also culminated in what is commonly referred to as the *"Fall of Saigon."*[9]

Before the executive order, the American legislature had rejected a request by President Ford to increase military aid for South Vietnam. The rejection came just before South Vietnam fell to Communist forces.[10] But what the roots of this policy decision were. What role President Ford played in the policy?

Another important question worth investigating is whether the President initiated the policy himself. It is plausible that such a policy decision might have been proposed by other players within the government. For this reason, we must grasp what prompted this sudden shift in United States foreign policy in Indochina.

We know from prior administrations that there had been a reluctance to abandon the war efforts in the region. What we do not know is the reason this sudden change occurred. All the same, we do not know who played a major role in the final decision to end the war. Thus, it is necessary to examine the final months, weeks, days, and even hours of the Vietnam Conflict.

REFUTING OTHER VIEWPOINTS

As I compiled this text, it was almost impossible to locate a compelling work, which might offer some insights as to why the Vietnam War ended. It is true; I have found numerous works that sought to explain the reason the Vietnam Conflict culminated the manner that it did. But such works have not really convinced me of what took place behind the scenes. After reading these materials, I am oft left with more questions than answers. Hence, the reason I have decided to compile this document.

I must admit that I was not able to examine the literature in depth. All the same, there is a good chance that I might have overlooked certain works regarding the war. Surely, I was able to evidence that various commentators have sought to explain the rationale that led to the end of the war. But by no means could I say that I have been able to review the literature thoroughly.

I will not explore theories or other explanations about the end of the conflict per se. But that position, in and of itself, is not a refutation of the literature. To be clear, I am not suggesting that I have reservations regarding the veracity of possible theoretical explanations concerning the war in terms of why it was fought, why it ended, and who ultimately won it.

My point is that I will not delve in the *"We-Win-Even-When-We-Lose"* Syndrome, as Espiritu Yen Le put it so eloquently.[11] As already noted, I reckon that many people have a particular viewpoint regarding the war. Here, however, I propose my own conceptual analysis as to what led to the end of the American involvement in Vietnam.

I must also point out that, in order to catch a glimpse into the potential motives that led to the unanticipated withdrawal from the region, it is paramount to espouse a scientific approach. By that understanding, I mean that we must come up with a theoretical tool, which would help us understand the nature of the withdrawal decision itself. This is why Allison's models are extremely helpful.

I rely on Allison's conceptual models for all the previously stated reasons. From this point forward, these models will serve as the ultimate intellectual guide, which would allow us to make sense of the American withdrawal from Vietnam. I will utilize the same strategy (or an approach akin to it), which this popular political scientist used in order to explain the Cuban Missile Crisis.[12]

A CONCEPTUAL FRAMEWORK

In 1969, Graham Allison proposed three conceptual models in order to assess the extent of salient governmental policies or actions during the Cuban Missile predicament. This political scientist wanted to ascertain the degree to which governmental activities had been based on certain policy rationales. The models Allison developed focused on governmental decision-making.

Allison notes that policy decisions are made from three perspectives. The first approach is identified as the rational-actor model. The second is the organizational behavior model. The third is the governmental politics.

Since we are only interested in ascertaining the nature of the decision to withdraw from Vietnam in the spring of 1975, let us explore only two of the models. I will explain the reason for that particular selection later in the text.

The first approach that is pertinent to the present queries is the *"Rational Actor"* Model. The second approach is the *"Governmental Politics"* Model. Right of the bat, let me say that I ignored the *"Organizational Process"* Model because it did not seem relevant to the issue at hand. The decision that led to the end of the war seemed emanated from individual players and not perforce at the organizational level.

Essentially, it must be acknowledged on the outset of our analysis that both Congress and the executive branch had a stake in the outcome of the Vietnam War. What they did or what they omitted from doing could be quintessential in helping us understand the last minute withdrawal decision. Other governmental entities apparently participated in the withdrawal decision. But it was not clear whether some specific governmental agency played a more prominent role in the policy making itself. There were no set actions taken by a particular organizational entity.

If anything, the decision to evacuate Saigon was chaotic. But this reality also suggested that the policy decision itself was disorganized and hasty, to say the least. As such, there was no need to explore the *Organizational Process Model* here.

Let us assess the making of the policy that led to the end of the war. Let us examine the role of Congress in creating the conditions necessary for the evacuation of American personnel from Saigon. Let us examine the role of the executive branch in making it impossible for Congress to yield to their demands. Let us focus on President Ford himself. To that extent, let us examine aspects of his policy decisions regarding the war.

HISTORY OF THE WITHDRAWAL POLICY

It is undeniable that the war officially ended on March 29, 1973.[13] But as outlined in previous chapters, many American soldiers were still present in Vietnam at the time. A number of them had been located in the Southern regions. Despite constant skirmishes between northern and southern Vietnamese fighters, views diverged as to whether the United States should continue its commitment to South Vietnam.[14]

In Washington, policy makers debated whether the American government should continue to support [unconditionally of course] the South Vietnamese regime.[15] On January 4, 1974, the United States Congress rejected President Richard Nixon's request for an increased military aid for South Vietnam.[16] But on August 8 of the same year, President Nixon resigned.

Because of the unanticipated presidential vacancy, Gerald R. Ford, Nixon's Vice President at the time, sworn-in as the 38th President of the United States. At that point, observers thought that there would be a change of policy in matters pertaining to the conduct of the Vietnam Conflict. But to most people's amazement, it was an unequivocal governmental continuity, at least from a foreign policy standpoint.

The question in most people's mind is why Ford took the same path as his predecessors on the matter of Vietnam. Let us examine the roots of that policy approach. Let us explore the origin of the policy rationale, which conclusively led to the end of the Vietnam War.

REQUESTING FUNDING

The newly installed President wasted no time to tackle the Vietnam problem. But he chose the same avenues that his predecessor used. President Ford sought to woo members of the legislature to approve a pending military aid package for the South Vietnamese regime.

On April 10, 1975, President Gerald Ford requested $722 million in military aid for South Vietnam. Not surprisingly, Congress also rejected that request. But since the Nixon administration, the American government had secretly promised South Vietnam more than $4 billion in reconstruction assistance before the war ends.[17] The problem is that the Ford administration could not honor this promise. There was a growing sense of a political turmoil in Washington. At that point, the American government had no choice but to completely withdraw its military personnel from Vietnam.[18]

There is no doubt that leaving the region altogether was not the course of action that the American government had envisioned in Vietnam. This was not a possibility that American officials even contemplated down the road. In so far, the issues I will debate in the next section will center on the reason a withdrawal was the policy that they implemented. Hence, it is indispensable to ascertain what instigated this sudden departure from a region that they had fought tooth and nail to maintain under control for so many decades.

It is also important to understand, at least at the intrinsic level, the reason the Ford administration could not honor its promise to the Southern regime. We must further ascertain who deserves the blame in this instance. We must understand the reason(s) the American government failed to galvanize the necessary political support for the war in the end.

The government's initiatives in Vietnam changed from fighting to fleeing. Unerringly, this was not the trademark of the American foreign policy at the time. What led to this stunning policy reversal? What led to this sudden change in military approach?

We could ask about the reason(s) that led the Americans to leave South Vietnam to fend for itself in the end of the conflict. In a frantic move, the government evacuated all personnel from the region. But short of surrendering to the Northern forces, America's actions perhaps led to the demise of the South Vietnamese stronghold (in the city of Saigon). But this event also marked the end of the conflict.[19] Let us explore in depth the situation [or situations] that led to this change of direction.

CHAPTER FOURTEEN

14. A CHANGE OF DIRECTION

THE AMERICANS HAD VOWED to rid Indochina of Communism. In the end, however, they chose to run from Vietnam. Their abrupt departure created a power vacuum, which made it even easier for both Communist ideologues and Communist sympathizers to take a hold in the region.

Between March and April 1975, the American government made a complete about-face regarding its foreign policy initiatives in Indochina. The pervading view is that Congress got the country out of this military quandary.[1] This being the case, the legislative branch yielded its power and resultantly prohibited any further combat role in the region.[2] As a result, President Gerald Ford had no more options, but to order American troops to leave.[3]

To this day, the atmosphere that led to this sudden change of direction is not well understood. As suggested in the previous chapter (*See* No Other Alternatives), an array of events [and actors] seemingly led to the change of foreign policy direction in Vietnam. But one event in particular had a cataclysmic effect on the policy choices of the American government. It could certainly be said that Congress' refusal to fund the war forced the American government out of Vietnam.

Unquestionably, the real reason Congress acted in such a manner is still elusive. Observers have speculated that the war had become so unpopular that it was about to change the political landscape at home. Political pressure, on the face of it, apparently led to the end of the war itself.

Regardless, historians largely attributed the collapse of South Vietnam and the fall of the capital (Saigon) to the fact that Congress did not approve the requested military aid to the South Vietnamese regime.[4] On the face of it, however, it could be said that this act alone does not positively refute the political aspects of the decision to pull out. But here, I will not delve into that particular aspect of the decision to withdraw all American troops from Vietnam.

Rather, let us explore the processes that led to the decision to cut off funding for the war. Using Allison's conceptual models, let us shed some lights on the decision-making mechanisms that culminated in the withdrawal policy. Again, let me note that this book does not poise itself as the sole approach to understanding the reason the war ended. There were other factors. But in the interest of time, I will not address all of them in the present analysis.

It seems logical to say that the United States found itself in a difficult position in Vietnam. The policy shambles during the conflict could be understood from various angles. Here, let us explore one particular aspect of the conflict. Let us examine the withdrawal decision itself. But let us do so primarily based on the models proposed by Allison.

CONGRESS AND THE WAR

The common belief is that the Vietnam War would not have ended if Congress did not withdraw its support for the war. Observers argue that with the enactment of the War Powers Act, the United States Congress was emboldened to assert its power in foreign policy decisions.[5] But is there any verity in that understanding?

This view had been echoed by various observers, both past and contemporary. In addition, the argument echoed by most analysts is that, Gerald Ford became the first President bound by the War Powers Resolution.[6] However, to all seeming, it could be said that the war in Vietnam was not going well, particularly when Gerald Ford, a person who spent his entire Washington career as a member of Congress building a reputation as a courteous and polite politician, became president.[7]

In the late 1960s, dissatisfaction with American policy in Vietnam had increased considerably.[8] The types of criticisms that were on average levied by democrats increased to the point where nearly two-thirds of the country had expressed their disapproval of war handling efforts.[9] Dissenting voices against the war were getting louder; they were regularly echoed in the media as well.

As noted in chapters ten and twelve, the media played an unprecedented role in bringing the war closer to home. They did so primarily via regular newscasts. Many people became convinced that the unremittingly and/or uncensored media coverage about the war changed the nature of American foreign policy initiatives during wartime.[10] This was irrefutably the case, notably during the war itself. A number of republicans were convinced that the Johnson administration refused to seek *"victory"* in Vietnam.[11]

The blame game that ensued weakened the government position and, to some extent, sabotaged any resemblance of a strategy to win the war. The major argument echoed by many democrats is that the war was too costly, in terms of both human and material resources. Other players within the government argued that the war was simply unwinnable.[12]

At that particular juncture, the government seemed devoid of a clear strategy either to achieve victory or to withdraw from the conflict. In 1963, the debate over a possible withdrawal from the conflict was settled.[13] But on the ground, the fighting spiraled into a nightmare and consumed many American lives. During that time, Vietnamese fighters sustained a number of casualties as well.[14]

At this particular juncture, the American government seemed incoherent as to the direction it envisioned in Vietnam. Policymakers appeared indecisive as to how they wanted to approach the conflict. Meanwhile, Congress hardened its tone and sought to flex its muscles as to how it wanted the war to be conducted.

In what many observers regarded as a Congressional overreach, Congress took a posture that weakened the American government's efforts to win the war. Some critics have even equated the situation as an attempt to slim down the powers of presidents. Nonetheless, Congress, in spite of all, rejected several aid requests for the war.[15] In May 1974, for instance, Congress rejected President Nixon's request to increase military aid to South Vietnam.

Subsequently, the Ford administration and Congress engaged in a fierce battle over additional emergency funding for Vietnam (in 1975 of course).[16] But as already illustrated, the legislators subsequently denied Ford's request on this front as well. A decision, which, many observers believed, effectively led to the end of the war. But could we use the models by Allison to shed some lights on these issues? Let us explore further.

ASSESSING THE MODELS

The concept evoked in Allison's famous publication was developed out a need to understand the Cuban Missile crisis. A failed attempt by the Central Intelligence Agency (commonly known as the CIA) to overthrow the Fidel Castro regime (in Cuba) marked a turning point in American foreign policy. [17] The Cuban missile crisis provided a glimpse into the policy mechanism of the American government at the time.

The Cuban crisis also provided the opportunity to understand the withdrawal decision in Vietnam. In order to grasp how the American government approached the Cuban missile crisis, Allison developed three conceptual models. [18] The author evaluated assumptions held by most analysts when they assess governmental and bureaucratic actions.

The three conceptual models are as follows: (1) the Rational-Actor Model, (2) The Organizational Behavior Model, and (3) The Governmental Politics Model. But in an attempt to understand the mechanisms of American governmental policy-making surgically, this inquiry focuses on two models: models one and three.

THE RATIONAL-ACTOR MODEL

Allison argues that occurrences in foreign affairs can be understood as the acts of nations. [19] The rational policy paradigm is comprised of five elements: (1) unit of analysis, (2) organizing concepts, (3) dominant inference patterns, (4) general propositions and assumptions, and (5) specific propositions. In the basis unit of analysis, policy is viewed as a national choice.[20]

In the rational-actor model, the understanding is that foreign affairs are conceived as actions chosen by a nation or nationals acting on behalf of a nation. In organizing concepts, a nation or a government is conceived as a rational, unitary decision-maker. [21] The government is the agent; it sets specific goals, which are widely based on utility function. Actions are generally tailored in response to a strategic problem.

In static selection, government makes a choice among other alternatives. The actions of the government are the chosen solutions to the problem. Such actions are *"a steady-state choice."*[22] When examining actions as rational choices, it could become evident that the actor has specific goals and objectives, which are normally informed by national security or national interests.

The actor has several options or courses of actions. However, the actor always takes into account the consequences of his or her actions. The enactment of a particular alternative will lead to a series of consequences. Such consequences could be both beneficial and costly. But this is relatively true in terms of an organization's strategic goals and objectives.[23]

Moreover, the rational actor must attempt to maximize choice. A rational choice is value maximizing. The actor makes the best possible choice in terms of his goals and objectives.

Another aspect of model one is the concept known as the dominant inference pattern. "If a nation performed a particular action, that nation must have had ends towards which the action constituted an optimal means." [24] The actor also makes some general propositions and assumptions.

ACTOR ASSUMPTIONS

The actor makes assumptions as to the likelihood of any particular action would results from a combination of nation's relevant values and objectives, perceived alternative courses of action, estimates of various sets of consequences, and net valuation of each set of consequences. Those propositions could lead to an *increase* in expected cost by *reducing* the likelihood that a certain course of action will be chosen. Alternatively, propositions may also lead to a *reduction* in expected cost by *increasing* the likelihood that a certain course of action will be chosen.

In specific propositions, deterrence is a key factor. The likelihood of attack may result from factors in general propositions. For instance, stable nuclear balance reduces the likelihood of nuclear attack.

Similarly, stable nuclear balance increases the probability of limited war. In the case of the Soviet Union (Soviet Force Posture), for instance, they choose force posture (e.g., Weapons & Deployment) as a value maximizing means of implementing soviet strategy.

Another aspect of the first model is the variants of rational policy model. The goal is to maximize value. The focus is on the national actor and his choice within a particular situation. National propensities or personality traits can be reflected in an *"operational code."*

These situations are principally concerned with certain objectives or special principles of action. This aspect focuses on individual leader or leadership groups as the actor whose preference function is maximized. It is important to recognize the existence of several actors. But the national actor is the one who wins in the end.

THE GOVERNMENTAL POLITICS MODEL

On the whole, in the bureaucratic political model, "The leaders who sit on top of organizations are not a monolithic group; rather, each is in his own right, a player in a central, competitive game.[25] Bargaining along regularizes channels among players; it is also positioned hierarchically within the government.[26]

In this instance, power is shared, as responsibility is devolved, by necessity of course.[27] Allison contends, *"Men share power."* They also differ concerning what must be done in a particular situation. These differences matter.[28] Because of certain divergences, policy makers may be pulled in different directions. The result is sometimes different from what anyone was aiming for.

The basic unit of analysis is that policy is based on political outcome. The organizing concepts entail players in positions. The actor is neither a unitary nation, nor a conglomerate of organization.[29] From this angle, the actor is a number of individual players. Put another way, groups of players constitute the agent for particular decisions/actions.

Positions define what players may do and/or must do. Allison notes that, "The advantages and handicaps with which each player can enter and play in various games stems from his position."[30] Moreover, players are also people (e.g., position and player that occupies it).

In parochial priorities, perceptions, and issues, question pertain to *"What is the issue?"* and *"What must be done?"* are determined based on the perspective from which such questions are posed.[31] Hence, there is a need to understand the pressures and baggage of the relevant organization.

There is a relationship between interests, stakes, and power. Games are played to determine outcomes.[32] The party that wants to win a battle with another bureaucracy must increase in power and influence.

POWER AND INFLUENCE

Power is an elusive blend of at least several elements, including bargaining advantages. That concept ordinarily includes the following trademarks: Formal authority and obligations, institutional backing, constituents, expertise, and status). But the leader must possess the necessary skills and the right amount of desire to engage in bargaining.

The leader must take advantages of these tools. That is to say, he or she must assess other players' perceptions of the first two ingredients.[33] In essence, if the party wants to avoid losing, it must do anything that would lead to the opposite outcome (i.e., winning). There might be other [added] incentives to win as well.

Another aspect to consider is the nature of the problems or the obstacles faced. Problems for dealing with the other players can be either narrower or broader than the overall or strategic problem(s) that the parties are trying to resolve. In many cases, some players could be unaffected by the magnitude of the situation. They might not feel a sense of urgency. But the leader must be aware of that conjecture as he or she initiates any bargaining.

Each player is concerned with the decision that must be made at a particular time. When it comes to the way of producing actions, bargaining is not a random affair. The structure of the encounter and the role of the major players are pre-determined by certain channels.

In this instance, action channels are "regularized ways of producing action concerning types of issues, structure the game by pre-selecting the major players, determining their points of entrance into the game."[34] In action as politics, outcomes are determined by the environment, pace of game, structure of game, rules of game, and rewards of game.

Allison notes that streams of outcomes are important governmental decisions or actions. Such outcomes "Emerge as collages composed of individual acts, outcomes of minor and major games, and foul-ups."[35] Actions are fabricated piece by piece.

Another important aspect is the dominant inference pattern. Every action performed by a nation can be approached as the outcome of bargaining activities among individuals and groups within the government. Within the concept of general propositions, actions and intentions are not intertwined. Put another way, an action does not presuppose an intention. Rather, it separates how individual with different intentions may contribute to outcomes.[36]

Based on the concept commonly understood as where a person stands may depend on where he/she sits, horizontal demands shape priorities, perceptions, and issues.[37] But within the notion of chiefs and Indians, vertical demands tend to shape priorities and actions. In specific propositions, deterrence is a key factor. For instance, the possibility of a nuke attack could depend on the probability that the decision to attack would emerge as the outcome of a bureaucratic activity.

CHAPTER FIFTEEN

15. APPLYING THE MODELS

AT THIS STAGE IN OUR discussions, let me emphasize that there exist fewer dissimilarities between the two chosen models. However, certain important nuances [and/or differences] are worth pointing out here. In model one, for example, the government acts as a unitary actor. Governmental decisions are made by a single individual. In this instance, the President, as the head of state, would make all policy decisions on behalf of the nation.

In model three, various individuals or groups of individuals determine outcomes.[1] Politics play a significant role in making decisions. But such decisions are mostly influenced or determined by outcomes. In model one, for instance, the decision maker is unitary, i.e., decisions are made by one individual. But in the third approach, decisions are made jointly by an array of actors.

Both approaches to decisions and actions are informed by the political realities on the ground. Decision outcomes are guided by compromise, competition between agencies or political entities within the government, coalition, and even confusion among government officials.

The president, as the ultimate decider, must take into account recommendations or advices offered by other players. In the second option, decisions are based on a multitude of factors, including the actors' capacity to come to a consensus, which, arguably, could be extremely difficult to do; the situation could be hard to decipher. But this could be more evident when it comes to issues that have important political ramifications both at home and abroad.

Moreover, priorities, actions, and outcome may differ based on the player positions and intentions. Since views generally diverge on any given issue, outcomes are based on political bargaining. Politics routinely play an important role in the decision making rational and process. But at this point in the debate, let us look at the extent to which Allison's models would apply to the Vietnam War.

ALLISON'S MODELS AND THE VIETNAM WAR

The two chosen models suggest that the decision to withdraw from Vietnam was motivated by political concerns. Based on the nature of our current discussions, one might say that this understanding, in and of itself, is no news, at least not for most observers. Nonetheless, the manner in which political issues impaired war efforts is not always clear. This is where the models are important.

The decision to withdraw from Vietnam was the outcome of the different directions that the actors within the American government wanted to take. In this case, the President was not the ultimate decision maker. He was not acting as a unitary entity within the American government.

The actions of the American government towards the end of the war consisted of a complete withdrawal from the region. In the event that is now known as the *"Fall of Saigon,"* President Gerald Ford ordered the evacuation of the last American embassy personnel in South Vietnam. One might say that this particular decision was not the result of the President's own desire. President Ford did not pressingly want to end the war in this manner. As far as I can see, I would say that the President was compelled to take this particular course of action.

Before the order to evacuate the region, Congress had rejected President Ford's request for emergency military aid for South Vietnam. Allison's third model, the *"Governmental Politics"* could explain President Ford's position and the reason he might have taken that path. Nevertheless, the next chapter examines the two models in depth. To reiterate, the goal is to decipher the making of that policy.

THE MAKING OF THE VIETNAM POLICY

The first model addresses the policy making process itself. As we try to understand President Ford's executive action during the war, it is worth noting some of the key players in the Ford administration's foreign policy. They include Henry Kissinger, Frank Church, James Schlesinger, Lt. Gen. Brent Scowcroft, John O. Marsh, Jr., John Gunther Dean, Martin A. Graham, Lehmann J. Wolfgang, Nguyen Van Thieu, and Max Friedersdorf.

The extent to which those players had a significant role in the withdrawal policy is not clear. But as some observers note, Gerald Ford inherited Richard Nixon's foreign policies and his foreign policy advisers.[2] President Ford had little room to interject his own approach into the polity of the government itself.

Against this background, it must be noted that as a former member of the House, President Ford was more prepared to direct foreign policy affairs than his critics would have admitted.[3] But what is also certain is that Henry Kissinger played a significant role in the policy direction of the American government at that level.[4] Thus, it could also be said that President Ford might have had little or no influence on the policy direction of the conduct of the war.

The presumption is that human beings are rational; they make decisions based on available alternatives. This case is particularly intriguing because President Ford, for some reason, chose a course of action that would be contrary to a rational decision maker. In this instance, a previous administration had made a similar request to Congress.

In the past, such an action yielded no result. Yet, the President wanted to proceed in the same path. In this respect, the relevant question worth ascertaining is why the President chose a similar approach.

There was a constant struggle between the President and Congress in the formation and the implementation of American policy.[5] Nevertheless, as the rational model posits, President Ford could not have chosen to do nothing. In this case, options were limited.

For example, in a telegram sent from the American embassy[6] in Cambodia to the State Department, on February 26, 1975, the message was loud and clear: "Danger was imminent," the message said. "I believe it is incumbent to alert you that we may now be approaching the crunch point," wrote ambassador Dean to President Ford.

"Even if we muddle through for another couple of weeks until the supplementary assistance can be voted on, the prospects facing us for the coming weeks are a continuation of the military setbacks and of the inability of the Khmers to organize their selves effectively to cope with the mortal danger facing them. The Americans on the scene are doing all we can to help the Khmers, but we cannot work miracles." Ambassador Dean echoed this understanding forcefully, I might say, in the telegram.

At that particular point in the conflict, the American government could not stop the Northern fighters from advancing towards the South. Since 1973, the war had officially ended. But the ambassador in Cambodia noted that the situation was deteriorating.

The only rationale option that the American government could adopt in Vietnam at that moment was a supporting role. At the time, they could only provide military assistance to the South Vietnamese government. The reason is that having combat troops on the battlefield was no longer a viable option for the Americans. That particular option was also off the table in Congress at the time.

Even the support role was no longer feasible. The problem is that Congress had previously rejected a request by the Nixon administration to provide military aid to South Vietnam. The rational-actor model could explain the reason the American government would choose to seek more funding. At first glance, one might say that this particular choice was the most rational choice.

The rational-actor framework posits that the President is the sole decision maker. The basic unit of analysis here is that policy is traditionally conceived as national choice. But there was a different picture in Washington.

THE PUSH BACK FROM CONGRESS

The decision to request additional military aid for South Vietnam and the ultimate order to evacuate the Vietnamese capital meant that the American government acted as a unitary rational nation. In spite of the fact that many people in the legislative branch had voiced their disapproval of the war and war efforts, President Ford took a stance that seemed contrary to the political reality at the time. In essence, the President acted as the agent of the nation, at least from the outside.

The war was unpopular domestically; few members of Congress approved it.[7] All the same, very few legislators would support the war in public. At that moment, in all likelihood, the national priority had shifted. There was also a shift in the policy direction the country (e.g., the direction that most of the country's leaders) wanted to take.

Nonetheless, President Ford seemed unconcerned by that reality. Evidently, President Ford sought to initiate a different policy direction in Vietnam. The policy was supported by the President's advisors, including the Secretary of State, Henry Kissinger himself.

The President wanted to seize on the humanitarian crisis that was developing in the region as a strategy to force Congress to reconsider its position. This was a well-calculated strategy. But it did not pay off, as the President and various members of his cabinet plausibly anticipated.

In a memorandum conversation recorded on March 4, 1975, Secretary Kissinger notes that "If some relief is not taken in Cambodia within the next two or three weeks, Cambodia is through." Secretary Kissinger further related to the President that Cambodia was an urgent issue.

On March 29, 1975, President Ford set the policy tone by announcing that there was an emergency, which necessitated the American government to adopt a different policy in Vietnam. As related in the Public Papers of President Gerald R. Ford, the President made a statement to the media, pointing out a humanitarian crisis in Vietnam.

The President ordered naval transport and contacted vessels to assist in the evacuation. The President also called upon other nations for corporation. He ordered that government resources should be made available to meet the immediate humanitarian needs.[8] These actions seemed on par with the notion that the government acted as a unitary agent and took actions in response to a strategic problem.

The President established the priorities of the government as national interests. He gave a news conference in which he pointed out that the American government had been helping South Vietnam. He also echoed that the government would continue to do so.

When asked whether he would accept a Communist takeover of South Vietnam, the President answered that he hoped that this would not take place. He also reiterated his goal, as a president, to avoid such a scenario.

The President acknowledged that his options were limited. He said that he hoped to avoid the mistakes of past administrations. This position suggests that President Ford perceived the American government's contribution to Vietnam as an optimal means. His actions also suggested that the government needed to make a steady choice among alternative outcomes, none of which was acceptable at the time.

When asked whether the American government miscalculated the intention of South Vietnamese willingness to resist the North Vietnam offensive, the President said the American government did not overestimate its actions in Vietnam; it certainly did not fail to understand the resilience of North Vietnamese to resist.

Other events, he argued, changed the situation on the ground. For example, he noted that the unilateral decision to withdraw from the war, led to the demise of South Vietnam. "A withdrawal decision by whom," the reporter further asked. The President answered that it was a decision by President Nguyen Van Thieu of Vietnam.

On April 11, 1975, President Ford sent draft bills authorizing additional military, economic, and humanitarian assistance for South Vietnam. The funds were needed for both the armed forces and for an eventual humanitarian evacuation.

The President urged immediate consideration and enactment of these measures. [9] Within the context of general propositions articulated in Allison's first model, the President sought to reduce the expected course of not supporting South Vietnam and increase the likelihood that Congress will follow his proposition.

THE TURNING POINT

On April 12, 1975, because of the serious deterioration of the military situation around the Cambodian Capital of Phnom Penh, and based on the recommendations of the United States ambassador to the Khmer Republic, the American government (via Gerald Ford himself) instructed the personnel of the American mission to leave Phnom Penh. But President Ford regretted that Congress had not acted on his request to continue providing the assistance necessary for the survival of the South Vietnamese government.

"The South Vietnamese government had clearly proven that it was worthy of our help," echoed President Ford. The President also noted that the American government wishes the Cambodian people the best. President

Ford further pointed out that he made numerous and vigorous diplomatic efforts to find a compromise settlement.

President Ford decided, with a heavy heart apparently, the evacuation of United States personnel out of the war zone. The reason he provided was that it encumbered to him the responsibility to guarantee the safety of all Americans who had served their country valiantly. He further echoed that despite the evacuation, the United States would continue to support the people of Cambodia. The President saluted the American Armed forces for the evacuation operation.[10]

On April 14, President Ford related to congress that the American government had a contingency plan to utilize the Armed Forces to assure the safe evacuation of United States Nationals from Vietnam. But in view of the deterioration of the situation, the President ordered the evacuation of American personnel from the country. He also noted that he ordered the military to proceed with the planned evacuation for the safety of American citizens.

The President acted within the purview of the section 4 of the war Powers Resolution. [11] For the evacuation, the American military commissioned 350 ground combat troops, which included the Marines, 36 helicopters, and supporting tactical air and command and control elements.

Among the rescued, there were 82 United States citizens, 35 third country nationals, and 159 Cambodians, including employees of the American government. The operation was ordered and conducted pursuant to the president's constitutional executive power and authority as commander-in-chief of the American Armed Forces.[12]

CHAPTER SIXTEEN

16. POLITICS AND POLICY MAKING

THE THIRD MODEL offers a political assessment of the withdrawal policy itself. Since the war lasted a long time, political interests and political issues carried over from one administration to the next. This model treats governmental decisions as a political struggle in which bargaining normally dictates outcomes.

In general, policy is viewed as political outcomes. Allison notes that in this model, multiple players with different policy goals compete. They tend to bargain over the substance and conduct of policy.

In this case, the main players were the executive and the legislative branches. Human rights and humanitarian issues have long been evoked as a ground for military intervention and aid to South Vietnam.[1] But Congress made it difficult for policy makers to claim a need for aid based on those criteria. Congress established the President and itself as the moral arbiters in domestic issues of other nations.[2]

Effectively, Congress wanted to end the Vietnam War by any means necessary. But the executive branch (i.e., President Gerald Ford) wanted to honor America's commitment to the South Vietnamese government.[3] But the outcomes did not favor what the President wanted and/or expected. It appeared as if the legislative branch played a more prominent role in the policy direction of the American government towards the end of the Vietnam Conflict.

The bureaucratic model posits that the leader who sits on top of an organization is not a monolithic group. From this perspective, the President himself does not represent the entire American government in foreign policy issues. Based on political traditions, Congress is the sole entity that delegates authority to the executive branch, especially in the area of conflicts and warfare.

As David Abshire and Ralph Nurnberger suggest, foreign policy decisions usually come from two governmental branches: Congress and the President.[4] From an historical standpoint, Congress, as usually, played a minimal role in governmental policy choices. Bearing in mind, political power continually shifted from the legislature to the executive branch. But since the mid-1970s, the role of congress has increased dramatically in this particular domain.

From 1950 to 1975, for instance, Congress accorded the executive branch wide latitude in decision-making. Presidents [and their aides] consistently determined the broad contours as well as the narrow specifics[5] of governmental policy.[6] Lawmakers were habitually content with this situation, even if it meant that one party would have control over two branches of government or complete dominance over American foreign policy initiatives.

There is another angle to consider here as well. For example, a president's authority to engage in foreign conflicts tended to increase when his party was in control of both chambers of Congress. Without a doubt, the Vietnam War changed that pattern.

CONGRESS AND FOREIGN POLICY

The debacle of the Vietnam Conflict led Congress no other alternatives, but to invest more attention to the creation of foreign policy plans and their subsequent implementations. In that sense, several Congressional members became important players in the policy itself. They also constituted the agent of policy decisions.

In 1973, Congress passed a comprehensive bill preventing further bombing of Cambodia.[7] By most assessments, this policy move was arbitrary. Of course, the executive branch was not pleased by that Congressional move. For instance, many members within the executive branch, including high-level cabinet members, charged that Congress was interfering with presidential powers. This light political clash was evidently on par with the notion of parochial priorities and perceptions and issues.

Undoubtedly, Congress had a different perception of the issues than the executive branch did. The outcomes of the Vietnam War suggest that the President could not reach a consensus with the different groups in Congress.

In a meeting with several special action groups in Washington, Henry Kissinger notes "The President's view is that we will not negotiate with Congress over the supplemental appropriation. We're not going to accept $75 million as a compromise. We'll accept only a sum that we think is acceptable to get the job done."[8]

In the end, however, the President seemed willing to negotiate with Congress for a compromise. In a memorandum of conversation regarding a three-year aid program discussion with several members of Congress, President Ford notes, "I feel an obligation. We must make a last massive effort to negotiate."[9]

During both the Nixon and the Ford administrations, Congress played a significant role in limiting the range of policy options of the executive branch. It later winded down the United States involvement in foreign conflicts, notably in Vietnam. This was a clear reversal of the Executive Power in foreign conflicts.

In the beginning of the Vietnam War, there were several supporters of the war. For instance, Democrats John Stennis of Mississippi and Gale McGee of Wyoming and Republicans Karl E. Mundt of South Dakota, John Tower of Texas, and the minority leader, Everett Dirksen of Illinois supported the war.

For good reasons, President Johnson always claimed that his war policy had bipartisan support.[10] With this mentality, it was widely believed that prominent members of Congress played a role in policy decisions. For instance, Senate majority leader, Mike Mansfield of Montana (The Foreign Relations Committee Chairman), J. William Fulbright of Arkansas (Committee Chairman), and Richard Russell of Georgia helped convinced President Johnson to escalate the war gradually.[11] Yet, when the conflict seemed uncontrollable, these prominent players were not able to maneuver other members of Congress in the President's direction. In the end, the American legislature did not lay down its arms.[12]

The Legislative body refuted President Ford's request without mercy. It was a stunning defeat for the President on a personal level. But it was also an unbearable embarrassment for the executive branch.

Within the context of actions as politics, outcomes can be informed by the environment. [13] The political environment during the war was not conducive for Congress to espouse a policy direction similar to the executive branch. There were too many opposition to the war for Congress to ignore the increasing public outcries against the conflict.

POLITICAL IMPLICATIONS

The Vietnam War was very unpopular. For many years, anti-war movements had been brewing in Washington. President Ford knew that he faced an uphill battle in Congress. That battle resembled the kinds of issues highlighted in Allison's approach to interest stakes and power.

As Julian Zelizer notes, it was an all-out-war in Washington.[14] Fulbright convened a televised hearing on the United States policy in Vietnam. "Legislators were outraged by the escalating violence," he noted.

Fulbright sought a legislation that would limit major military escalation. Several figures, including George F. Kennan and General James M. Gavin, testified that America's preoccupation with Vietnam was having a negative effect on other foreign policy initiatives. Fulbright further noted, "America was not responding to its global obligations."

The argument is that America had committed too many resources to Vietnam. All the same, Defense secretary, Dean Rusk, faced tough questions from senators. He was asked what America's objectives were in the war; the legislators also asked him how long the war would last.[15] But he could not provide a clear answer.

Senator Wayne Morse confronted the former American ambassador to Saigon, General Maxwell Taylor, and told him that it would not take long before the American people repudiate the war in Southeast Asia. But Taylor also argued that such a situation would unmistakably benefit Hanoi [in North Vietnam].

There was a growing anti-war sentiment in the senate since the days of Johnson.[16] The majority of democrats would not keep funding the war much longer. President Nguyen Van Thieu knew that.

In a message from the Deputy Chief of Mission in Vietnam (Lehmann) to the Ambassador to Vietnam (Martin) in Washington, the message was unequivocal. It suggested that the situation was deteriorating both in Vietnam and in Washington. "The chances of getting congressional support were grim," he noted.

At that point, a compromise could not be reached between President Ford and Congress. Individual players in both chambers of the legislature seemed hunted by the demons of the past. The streams of outcomes dwindled and the policy options of the government predetermined by certain channels.

Anti-war critics blamed Congress for ceding too much power to the executive branch, while supporters of the war blamed Congress for what they perceived as easy compromise. [17] Within that context, reaching a consensus for the military aid requested by President Ford appeared extremely difficult.

EXTENT OF THE MODELS

There is no doubt that the rational-actor model could help us understand the reason President Ford sought support from Congress, even though the chances of success were slim. The President had some specific goals and objectives that he wanted to accomplish. Despite the fact that Congress had rejected the executive branch's previous requests, President Ford seemed unaffected by that reality.

It could be argued that the President, acting as a rational actor, had his own goals and objectives. To a high degree, such ambitions were informed by national security or national interests. But the reality is that President Ford's ambitions were also muffled by the same interests.

The rational-actor model provides a clear picture about the making of the policy to request additional military aid for South Vietnam. In this instance, the policy was primarily driven by the executive branch. Its failure was also the result of the executive branch's incapacity to rally other players, notably members of the legislative branch, into its camp.

When the policy is driven by one individual, in this instance, President Gerald Ford himself, the rational actor model is best suited to explain the reason for the policy. Naturally, there are pros and cons to this approach. As Weissman Stephen notes, Congress customarily approaches foreign policy from a culture of deference. [18] Unlike the executive wing of government, Congress has certain set of norms and beliefs, customs and institutions that legitimate its power.[19]

The idea that policies must have bipartisan supports is often evoked as the way to do business in Congress. Arguably, this view also limits moral competitions between democrats and republicans. Moreover, this understanding is simply misguided when it comes to foreign policy initiatives. From this angle, a rational actor model would make perfect sense to explain the reason President Ford acted the manner that he did.

It could also be said that too many players may clog the policymaking process. A negative aspect to this approach is that it may lead to less compromise when compromise is needed. For example, the myth of presidential superiority may strengthen congress culture of bipartisanship, which in turn may hamper the president's initiative. This reality was evident during the Vietnam War. For these reasons, foreign policy during wartime could be best understood from a bureaucratic model approach.

LESSONS FROM THE VIETNAM DEBACLE

Clifford Hackett argues that the war served as education for congress about the opportunities and the traps of sharing foreign policy decisions with the president.[20] But Vietnam also broke the dangerous trance of presidential domination in foreign policy.[21] Incontestably, the Vietnam War changed the relationship between the two branches of government.

Robinson James further notes that because of the Vietnam debacle, Congress now enjoys an increasing role in policymaking.[22] Congress plays a role in various aspects of the policy-making process. Nonetheless, the role of the American Legislature in the country's foreign policy initiatives is not egregiously pervasive. Such a role is principally in the recommendation and prescription of the decision process.

Recommendations of important measures are initiated by the executive branch, rather than the legislative. But the scope of congressional influence varies with the constitutional provisions governing the making of conduct of foreign relations. There is always room for compromise.

I must admit it; a rational-actor model only takes into account the role of the chief, in this case, the President. But such an approach also tends to marginalize the role of the other players. By contrast, the bureaucratic politics model is more inclusive, particularly in terms of the different elements or actors exerting an influence on the policy itself.

No doubt, the decision to request military aid from Congress was instigated or perhaps conceived at the unitary level. But the policy rationale could not be explained from that angle alone. The bureaucratic model, on the other hand, provided a more in-depth assessment of the origin of the policy and the role of the different governmental players in the policy outcomes.

FINAL WORDS

THE VIETNAM WAR is perhaps one of the most resounding military and/or foreign policy ventures in American history. No doubt, this military scuffle did not end like previous conflicts. To this day, the outcome of the war is still uncertain.

Officially, the American government never claimed to have won the war; but they never admitted defeat in Vietnam either. From most people's vantage point, no one truly won the war itself, though they recognize that there were a few setbacks here and there. Still, it must also be said that this is relatively the case as far as winners and losers are concerned.

On other fronts, there is an argument to be made that the Vietnamese people were victorious in the conflict. At the end of the day, the Northern fighters were able to rebuff American dominion in Vietnam. All the same, Communism became the norm in Laos, Cambodia, and Vietnam, not to mention that Communism took a hold in various parts of Indochina.

Truth be told, the extent of Communist ideologies did not branch out in the entire East Asia, as most people anticipated. Still, the Americans did not win the prize that they sought in Vietnam. Looking at the conflict from these angles, the argument could be made that the Americans did lose the Vietnam War.

As outlined in this text, most observers are not of the opinion that the Americans lost the war itself. That is to say, the debate is still brewing about which party ultimately prevailed in Vietnam. Not forgetting that, assessing the issues from an objective lens was also a daunting task. Hence, the views articulated here only reflect my perception of the issues.

The Vietnam War is among the most commented conflicts in American military history. Presently, there are more than 30,000 books in print regarding the war. Many book retailers, which include brick and mortar establishments and online bookstores,[1] have shelved an array of published materials about the war.

Most people have an understanding about the nature of the Vietnam War. The conflict is so popular that few people need a particular expertise or academic background to discuss it. Comments about the war often take many forms. But accuracy is not always at the highest level.

Vietnam is a very touchy subject in American society. People often have mixed feelings about the reason the war was fought. As insinuated earlier, it is also unclear who finally won the conflict. Few people agree as to the reasons the war started and the reason it ultimately ended.

Granted, I must admit that deciphering the reason the war ended could be hard to explain. But this is generally the case, when it comes to the actions taken by the American government. To reiterate, there was no clear winner declared. This reality clearly invites speculations about the war itself.

While the war was fought thousands of miles away, its effects could be felt at home. The conflict divided friends and family members in many places, including in big cities and local communities. People held, and, assumably, still hold, different views about the war and its benefits, both at home and abroad. For these reasons, talking or even writing a book about Vietnam is often the subject of intense, at times, passionate debates.

The present work was compiled from a layperson's perspective. The views highlighted herein were not designed as a tool to gauge the after effects of the war; this work is not a rewrite of history. The ideas evoked in the text were not designed to advocate in favor of one particular side to the detriment of another. Put another way, the goal was to present an objective assessment about the events that led to the end of the conflict itself.

WRITING ABOUT VIETNAM

Why was it necessary to write a book about Vietnam? From a policy standpoint, the types of information that are currently available about the war are ambiguous. One might even say that there is a lack of objectivity in the literature.

As previously echoed, people have different perspectives about when, why, and how the United States was involved in Indochina. That type of bias is often reflected in the present literary discourse. In this book, I wanted to offer an alternative to counter slanted views.

Evidently, this volume is not a typical text regarding the Vietnam War per se. The ideas echoed here were specifically designed to be academically oriented. For sure, the views expressed throughout this text were geared towards a particular aspect of the war. But this work does not poise itself as the ultimate authority on the subject.

It should be apparent by now that this volume only focused on the events, which led to the end of the war. The ideas I developed in the text did not vitally expand on the intricacies of the conflicts or the reasons the war started. This book attempted to explicate possible reasons the Vietnam War eventually ended in the manner in which it abruptly did. But the crux of my analysis primarily centered on the policy rationale for the withdrawal decision itself.

I examined the origin of the final decision in Vietnam from a policy-making lens. In my arguments, I sought to retrace the events that led to the frantic evacuation from Saigon. This event is often regarded as the most relevant moment in the conflict, which culminated to a symbolic end of the military hostilities. The Saigon evacuation is the best-known event about the Vietnam War. Irrefutably, this moment undoubtedly marked the end of American involvement in the region. This event was also the center of my examination here.

Plenty of books do a good job explicating the history of the Vietnam Conflict. This volume is not such a book. The ideas I highlighted in this text would not perforce elucidate any misgivings about the war. I did not intend to argue in favor of one side to the detriment of another.

That being noted, I would argue that the events that led to the end of the war were clearly the results of a guided decision by the Ford administration. This was not a haphazard policy venture. That decision was clearly informed by a strong policy rationale. My objective was to decipher that rationale at its most basic level.

In order to understand the reason such a policy was implemented, it was important to get a good grasp of the circumstances that led to its adoption in the first place. Here, I sought to help the reader understand the policymaking mechanisms that ostensibly led to this untimely evacuation from the hilltop of an American embassy in the city of Saigon.

ASSESSING THE LITERATURE

As already mentioned throughout this manuscript, a litany of publications exists about the Vietnam War. But the literature on the subject can be extremely convoluted. It being understood to be the case, at least in most instances, it could also be said that most of the information that are available about the war might not be sufficient to help any inquirer understand the reason American helicopters were scrambling to get people out of Saigon on D-day. Given this circumstance, it was pertinent to evaluate the policy ramifications of the withdrawal itself.

To echo an argument adumbrated throughout the text, most books on the subject are opinion pieces. Some are narratives, which relate commonly know events. These works tend to reflect on views, which had been expressed by either one individual or several person(s).

Many of these works are often based on the perceptions of those who experienced Vietnam one way or another. Such works do not ineluctably reflect the reality or the possible realities that American decision-makers faced outside of the battleground (i.e., in Washington). I sought to complement those works in the present literary demarche.

What I am saying is that few works explored the political theater that seemed to exist in Washington during the war. Here, I sought to bridge that gap. This text offered the reader the opportunity to evaluate the policy mechanism that clearly led to the end of the Vietnam Conflict.

The literature is filled with materials that offer a good summary of the war. The Internet is also saturated with blog posts or other items by either people who experienced the war directly or writers who tend to relate the experiences of others. Those works, however useful for a quick summary of the events, can be inaccurate and unreliable for an in-depth examination of the conflict itself. This book did not rely, at least not exclusively, on these types of materials.

The present work offered an examination of a number of compilations about Vietnam. I explored several selected scholarly works about the conflict. The text also featured several reflections regarding personal accounts about the war. Nonetheless, this text did not rely on book reviews or other examinations from previously publicized accounts about Vietnam.

In order to compile this book, I consulted reputable search engines, databases, and popular academic journals. The goal was to offer an academic approach to the subject. Simply put, this text sought to evaluate the issues as accurately as possible.

Let me also reecho that this book was not the result of an academic inquiry per se. The text is the compilation of a series of essays I completed for a class project. To restate, this work was not designed as a means to substitute any scholarly contribution about the topic. This book is a hybrid between a compilation of essays and a research paper.

No doubt, this opus is different from the class project I related in the preface segment. This work is a more polished product. The goal was to compile a book that would be worthy of your intellectual curiosity. But determining whether I succeeded in this endeavor is up to you (i.e., the reader).

I must say it; I had a lot of fun writing this book. I learned a lot from the topic of Vietnam. I sincerely hope that you had a similar experience reading this paperback.

NOTES

Preface

[1] By that, I mean "hands-on" or practical experience.

[2] I was born in 1975, more specifically during the month of April.

—

A Class Project

[1] At the time, I was in graduate school; I was completing a Master's degree in political science.

[2] This course took place at Villanova University.

[3] I am referring to a very popular Political Science program at Villanova University.

[4] I am referring to Southeast Asia, more specifically Indochina.

[1] The author of the models (Allison T. Graham) is a famous political scientist.

[2] These entities constitute the major sources I will cite throughout this document.

[3] American had a large Embassy in the region. That embassy was the last sovereign territory, which was evacuated in what seemed like an impending doom. This event is the essence of the text.

—

Chapter One

[1] Olson, *Historical Dictionary of the 1960s*, 466.

[2] Olson, *Historical Dictionary of the 1960s*.

[3] Haley, *Congress and the Fall of South Vietnam and Cambodia*, 98.

[4] Haley, *Congress and the Fall of South Vietnam and Cambodia*.

[5] This includes both Democrats and Republicans.

[6] See chapters nine, eleven, and thirteen to learn more about the effects of the withdrawal decision.

[7] Haley, *Congress and the Fall of South Vietnam and Cambodia*.

—

Chapter Two

[1] By that statement, I mean that Congress has the authority [or the duty] to check and balance the other branches of government. Its intrusion in foreign policy initiatives during Vietnam was clearly the manifestation of that prerogative.

[2] Ganzel, "The Vietnam War and Rural America."

[3] Brinkerhoff and Wallechinsky, "How Much Does a U.S. War Cost?"

[4] Ibid.

[5] Daggett, "Military Operations: Precedents for Funding Contingency Operations in Regular or in Supplemental Appropriations Bills."

—

Chapter Three

[1] Olson, *Historical Dictionary of the 1960s*, 466.

[2] I use the terms Laos and Lao People's Democratic Republic interchangeably.

[3] Pdoggbiker, "What Sets The Vietnam Veteran Apart From All Other Wars by Jack Smith."

[4] Ibid.

[5] Ibid.

[6] Ibid.

[7] Hanson and Beaton, "Vietnam War Facts, Stats and Myths."

[8] Ibid.

[9] Ibid.

[10] Ibid.

[11] Ibid.

[12] Ibid.

[13] Turse, *Kill Anything That Moves*.

[14] Ibid., 2.

[15] mapsofworld.com, "Where Is Vietnam: Vietnam Location in World Map."

[16] Nationsonline.org, "Viet Nam - Vietnam - Country Profile - Việt Nam, Asia."

[17] Ibid.

[18] worldatlas.com, "Where Is Viet Nam? Where Is Viet Nam Located in The World? Viet Nam Map."

[19] Ibid.

[20] Brigham, "Battlefield Vietnam: A Brief History."

[21] The Truman doctrine is the notion that America would provide money and military equipments to nations that sought to eradicate Communist influence onto their lands.

[22] Jordan et al., *American National Security*, 2009.

[23] CNN, "Vietnam War Fast Facts - CNN.com."

—

Chapter Four

[1] The reason the United States sought to prevent Vietnam from becoming communities was laid out is the concept known as the "Domino Theory." This is the notion that if Vietnam became Communist, the entire continent would become Communist.

[2] Brigham, "Battlefield Vietnam: A Brief History."

[3] Ibid.

[4] Alpha History, "South Vietnam under Ngo Dinh Diem."

[5] Brigham, "Battlefield Vietnam: A Brief History."

[6] Jordan et al., *American National Security*, 2011, 375.

[7] Ibid.

[8] Brigham, "Battlefield Vietnam: A Brief History."

[9] CNN, "Vietnam War Fast Facts - CNN.com."

[10] The Tonkin incident is when North Vietnamese men attacked a United Vessel, which had been patrolling in the Gulf of Tonkin.

[11] Congress passed the "Gulf of Tonkin Resolution," which authorized the President to take military action in Vietnam.

—

Chapter Five

[1] After the Gulf of Tonkin incident, the U.S. became deeply embroiled in the conflict. This event transpired when North Vietnamese fighters fired on a United States destroyer. The destroyer had been patrolling the area at the time. Immediately, President Lyndon Johnson sought congressional authority to wage war with North Vietnam. In a joint resolution, Congress gave President Johnson the power to engage in a military conflict in the region.

[2] CNN, "Vietnam War Fast Facts - CNN.com."

[3] Ibid.

[4] The term POW means "Prisoner Of War." The term MIA means "Missing In Action."

[5] CNN, "Vietnam War Fast Facts - CNN.com."

[6] The Viet Cong: who were they? They were the military branch of the National Liberation Front (NLF). They were commanded by the Central Office for South Vietnam. Learn more about the Vietcong. PBS, "Battlefield: Vietnam (Guerrilla Tactics)."

[7] CNN, "Vietnam War Fast Facts - CNN.com."

[8] Containment is the notion that America should stop the spread of Communism by keeping Communist influence contained. The containment doctrine presupposes that countries like the Soviet Union and China in their attempt to agitate Western democracies with socialist ideas. Within the context of Cold War strategies, Harry S. Truman is credited with the evolution of the doctrine in late 1940s, as a response to crises in turkey and Greece.

[9] The term "Manifest Destiny" was coined by American writer John L. O'Sullivan, in 1845. The term could be understood from two angles: Domestic and Foreign Policy. From a domestic policy standpoint, the term encompasses the idea that Americans have a God-given mission to expand westward, to occupy a continental nation, and to extend American constitutional influence to enlightened people. The foreign policy angle denotes that the Unites States has an obligation to push democracy and nation building throughout the world (Jones, "American Manifest Destiny.").

[10] The Truman Doctrine is the notion that the United States must send money, equipment, or military force to places threatened by a rise of Communism (Kelly, "6 Foreign Policy Doctrines You Should Know.").

[11] Defense Casualty Analysis System, "Defense Casualty Analysis System Reports - Vietnam Conflict Casualty Summary."

—

Chapter Six

[1] Gorner, "Life Of A Tunnel Rat."

[2] Ibid.

[3] Rottman, *Viet Cong Fighter*, 22.

[4] Hochgesang, Lawyer, and Stevenson, "War & Peace: Media and War."

[5] Rottman, *Viet Cong Fighter*.

[6] Ibid., 22.

[7] I am referring to those branded as Communists.

[8] I am referring to those fighters in the Northern regions.

[9] This was true on both sides of the conflict.

[10] history.com, "My Lai Massacre - Vietnam War."

[11] Ibid.

[12] The understanding is that troop morale was very low after a North Vietnamese offensive, which led to the death of several military personnel. Coincidentally, the same company that sustained heavy casualties from the South Vietnamese offensive was sent in a search and destroy mission in the My Lai region. Learn more about the My Lai incident from History.com. Ibid.

[13] history-world, "Vietnam War Statistics."

[14] National Archives, "Statistical Information about Casualties of the Vietnam War."

[15] The New York Times, "How Many Suicides by Vietnam Vets?"

[16] James, Susan Donaldson, "Suicide Rate Spikes in Vietnam Vets Who Won't Seek Help."

[17] history-world, "Vietnam War Statistics."

[18] Ibid.

—

Chapter Seven

[1] In Iraq, between 2006 and 2011, American military forces fought a guerrilla-type war, which had many similarities with the Conflict.

[2] Christopher, "Kissinger, Ford, and Congress," 440.

[3] Christopher, "Kissinger, Ford, and Congress."

[4] Ibid., 440.

[5] Christopher, "Kissinger, Ford, and Congress."

[6] The Paris Peace agreement was signed on January 27, 1973. But it was nothing but a temporary truce, rather than a genuine peace accord. Learn more at: Defense Casualty Analysis System, "Defense Casualty Analysis System - Vietnam War - Conflict Casualties."

[7] Christopher, "Kissinger, Ford, and Congress."

[8] The term "Vietnamization" was coined by President Richard Nixon in an attempt to demonstrate that the South Vietnamese regime could defend itself in the conflict.

[9] Christopher, "Kissinger, Ford, and Congress," 441.

[10] Ibid., 442.

[11] Ibid.; Joes, *The War for South Viet Nam, 1954-1975*.

—

Chapter Eight

[1] I am referring to Indochina in particular.

[2] DeLeon, "Opinion."

3 In 1992, the New York Times published an op-ed piece, which was very critical of the way Bill Clinton avoided being drafted into the War in 1969. (The New York Times, "Bill Clinton's Vietnam Test.")

[4] Lardner and Romano, "Washingtonpost.com: At Height of Vietnam, Bush Picks Guard."

[5] Seelye, "The 2004 Campaign."

[6] The Washington Times, "Biden's Draft Deferments Equal Cheney's during Vietnam War."

[7] The Swift Boat Veterans challenged John Kerry's military record in Vietnam. They put into question whether, at the time candidate, John Kerry, deserved his combats medals.

[8] In a poll conducted by the University of Pennsylvania National Annenberg Election Survey showed that a number of Americans thought the "Swiftboat"

veterans had a huge impact on their perception regarding Mr. Kerry service record. http://www.pollingreport.com/wh04misc2.htm

[9]Embassy, "Chronology."

[10] The American Presidency Project, "William J. Clinton: Remarks Announcing the Normalization of Diplomatic Relations With Vietnam."

[11] Associated Press, "U.S. Expected To Restore Full Relations With Vietnam | Deseret News."

[12] Peck, "Bill Clinton Visits Vietnam to Mark 20th Anniversary of Ties."

[13] Ibid.

[14] As cited on the website (Ibid.)

[15] On May 25, 2012, President Barack Obama started a program, which will commemorate the 50th anniversary of the Conflict. The program will run between May 25, 2012 and November 11, 2025. The goal is to "honor and give thanks to a generation of proud Americans who saw our country through one of the most challenging missions we have ever faced" (CNN, "Vietnam War Fast Facts - CNN.com.")

—

Chapter Nine

[1] DeLeon, "Opinion."

[2] See the psychological effects of the war by Josh Hochgesang, Tracye Lawyer, and Toby Stevenson to learn more. Hochgesang, Lawyer, and Stevenson, "War & Peace: Media and War."

[3] This term was originally coined by President Dwight D. Eisenhower, whom, ironically, was among the instigators of the Vietnam War. But as a former military himself (Five-star general during world War II), Eisenhower's argument centers on the premise that a relationship (generally an informal alliance) between a nation's military and the industry that supplies that military its arms could be detrimental to that country's public policy. History.com Staff, "Eisenhower Warns of Military-Industrial Complex - Jan 17, 1961."; also see Gee, "Who Really Killed President John F. Kennedy and Why."; Birney, "Kennedy & Merton."; Douglass, *JFK and the Unspeakable*..

[4] McMahon, "Changing Interpretations of the Vietnam War."

[5] The wars in Afghanistan and Iraq are among the most recent American military involvement in conflicts. Between 2006 and 2011, there was a phobia of Vietnam-like-Iraq in America. Many people feared that Iraq would turn in the next Vietnam. Just like in Vietnam, a few years into the war, American casualties steadily increased with no end in sight.

[6] Learn more about the debate by visiting these websites: Analysts Discuss Possible Iraq-Vietnam Parallels. PBS NewsHour, "Analysts Discuss Possible Iraq-Vietnam Parallels."; Parallels Between Iraq and Vietnam. Chapman, "Parallels Between Iraq and Vietnam."; A True Parallel between Vietnam, Iraq: Vitriol. Carpenter, "A True Parallel between Vietnam, Iraq."; Bush Aide Sees a Parallel Between Vietnam and Iraq. Stout, "Bush Aide Sees a Parallel Between Vietnam and Iraq."

[7] See a dissenting viewpoint regarding the parallel between Vietnam and Iraq. Stop Comparing Iraq to the Vietnam War. Stur, "Stop Comparing Iraq to the Vietnam War."

[8] The term bi-partisan denotes that both Democrats and Republicans participated in the decision to go to war in Vietnam.

[9] H.J. RES 1145. Joint resolution of Congress dated August 7, 1964. Ourdocuments.gov, "Our Documents - Tonkin Gulf Resolution (1964)."

[10] Ibid

[11] It is worth noting that the resolution did not convey, on its face, an authorization to a large-scale war in Vietnam. Analysts debate whether the document authorized the extent of the Conflict (infoplease.com, "Tonkin Gulf Resolution.").

[12] Office of the Historian, Bureau of Public Affairs and United States Department of State, "U.S. Involvement in the Vietnam War: The Gulf of Tonkin and Escalation, 1964 - 1961–1968 - Milestones - Office of the Historian."

—

Chapter Ten

[1] Trinity College, "Media."

[2] Hallin, *The Uncensored War.*

[3] Ibid., 3.

[4] I am referring to the many movies that have been made about Vietnam.

—

Chapter Eleven

[1] Haley, Congress and the Fall of South Vietnam and Cambodia.

[2] Haley, *Congress and the Fall of South Vietnam and Cambodia*, 99.

[3] Ibid.

[4] Several people resisted the Vietnam War. See Democracy Now!, "Military Jailing Vietnam War Resisters 40 Years After They Refused to Serve."; See Block,

"Muhammad Ali Risked It All When He Opposed The Vietnam War."; See Schechter, "Opinion."

[5] The end of the War is marked by the evacuation from Saigon. This even is known as "The Fall of Saigon."

Chapter Twelve

[1] Joes, *The War for South Viet Nam, 1954-1975*.

[2] What does the term "Containment" means? I discussed this term in the first chapter. But let us explore this term further in order to cater a good gasp of its significance in the present instance.

[3] Containment is the notion that the U.S. must oppose the expansion of Soviet influence in Western Europe and East Asia. To achieve this goal, the U.S. can use different means, including politics, economic, and military avenues.

[4] O'Connor and Sabato, *American Government*, 726.

[5] Haley, *Congress and the Fall of South Vietnam and Cambodia*.

[6] The concept known as the "Power of the Purse," is often used in scholarly circles to illustrate the capacity of the United States Congress to determine the direction of both domestic and foreign policies. Congress has the power to appropriate funding for governmental projects. Accordingly, they decide when, how, why, and to whom money is appropriated and allocated.

[7] In the article "Congress' Power of the Purse," Stith Kate examined the constitutional role of Congress to exert oversight on governmental spending. The author also examined the executive's limitation and restrain in their ability to raise and spend funds (Stith, "Congress' Power of the Purse.").

[8] Stalnaker, "A Theory of Conditionals."

Chapter Thirteen

[1] This period in the American history was marked by other social problems, including the civil rights movement. It was also a period of an unprecedented youth rebellion.

[2] Barringer, "The Anti-War Movement in the United States."

[3] Ibid.

[4] Riggs, "Vietnam War."

[5] Kenny Rogers, "Who Were U.S Presidents during the Vietnam War?"

[6] Bradford, *A Companion to American Military History.*

[7] "Congress and the White House in the Vietnam War."

[8] The Encyclopedia of American Political history (2010) notes that the War was profoundly shaped by American politics; the war also shaped American politics in the process.

[9] Aneja and Rothman, "Eyewitness to the Fall of Saigon."

[10] PBS "Biography: 38. Gerald R. Ford." American Experience. PBS, "38. Gerald R. Ford . The Presidents . WGBH American Experience | PBS."

[11] Espiritu, "The 'We-Win-Even-When-We-Lose' Syndrome."

[12] Graham T. Allison developed the conceptual models as a means to analyze the Cuban Missile Crisis. Allison used the crisis as a case study to understand governmental decision-making processes.

[13] Anderson, *Shadow on the White House.*

[14] Robertson, *Encyclopedia of U.S. Political History.*; Felzenberg, "Ford, Gerald R."

[15] Congress and the White House in the War (2006)

[16] ibid

[17] Jespersen, "The Bitter End and the Lost Chance in Vietnam."

[18] Greene, "Essays on Gerald Ford and His Administration."; Miller Center, "Gerald Ford: Impact and Legacy."; Friedman, "Gerald Ford, The Mayaguez Incident, And The Post-Imperial Presidency."

[19] Whalen, *The House and Foreign Policy.*

—

Chapter Fourteen

[1] Zelizer, "How Congress Got Us Out of Vietnam."

[2] Zanolli, "What Happened When Democrats in Congress Cut Off Funding for the Vietnam War?"

[3] Congress exerted the power of the purse to prevent further American military involvement in Vietnam.

[4] Zanolli, "What Happened When Democrats in Congress Cut Off Funding for the Vietnam War?"

[5] Bresler, "The Specter of Vietnam."

[6] Friedman, "Gerald Ford, The Mayaguez Incident, And The Post-Imperial Presidency."; Mascaro, "The Road to War."

[7] Friedman, "Ford, Gerald (Administration of)."

[8] Herman, "Who Owns the Vietnam War?"

[9] Guttmann, "Protest against the War in Vietnam."

[10] Bullard, "The Mercurial Role of the U.S. Media in Wartime."

[11] Guttmann, "Protest against the War in Vietnam."

[12] Ibid.

[13] Bradford, "History Matters - Vietnam Withdrawal Plans."

[14] Ibid.

[15] According to a series of documentary and films about American Presidents (American Experience), Congress sought to regain control of over the war powers of the executive branch through the power of the purse. Towards the end of the war in Vietnam, Congress denied the Ford administration's request for additional emergency funding for South Vietnam. This was a blatant attempt by Congress to limit the president's power in matters of foreign policy.

[16] Zelizer, "How Congress Got Us Out of Vietnam."

[17] On April 1961, Cuban exiles, aided by the American government launched an invasion in Cuba. The invasion ultimately failed and brought embarrassment to the country and threatened long-term security interests of the United States in the region.

[18] In 1969, Graham T. Allison published an article titled: Conceptual models and the Cuban Missile Crisis. In this piece, the author developed three models of government to explain policy decisions during the Cuban missile crisis.

[19] Allison, "Conceptual Models and the Cuban Missile Crisis," 693.

[20] The term nation choice denotes decisions that are taken with the goal of furthering national interests.

[21] Allison, "Conceptual Models and the Cuban Missile Crisis," 694.

[22] Ibid.

[23] Allison, "Conceptual Models and the Cuban Missile Crisis."

[24] Ibid., 694.

[25] Ibid., 707.

[26] Ibid.

[27] The notion of governmental politics suggests that politics play an important in the decision making process.

[28] Allison, "Conceptual Models and the Cuban Missile Crisis," 707.

[29] Ibid., 708.

[30] Ibid., 709.

[31] Allison, "Conceptual Models and the Cuban Missile Crisis."

[32] Ibid., 710.

[33] Allison, "Conceptual Models and the Cuban Missile Crisis."

[34] Ibid., 710.

[35] Ibid.

[36] Ibid., 711.

[37] Allison, "Conceptual Models and the Cuban Missile Crisis."

—

Chapter Fifteen

[1] In this model, individuals play a more prominent role because of the organizational structure.

[2] Greene, "Essays on Gerald Ford and His Administration."

[3] Ibid.

[4] Jespersen, "Kissinger, Ford, and Congress."

[5] Coleman and Keefer, "Foreign Relations of the United States, 1969–1976, Volume X, Vietnam, January 1973–July 1975 - Office of the Historian."

[6] John Gunther Dean was Ambassador to Cambodia during the evacuation.

[7] Carson, "Beyond the Solid South."

[8] Statement announcing humanitarian assistance for Refugees in the Republic of Vietnam (p. 406) (163). United States Government Printing Office, "Public Papers of the Presidents of the US, Gerald R. Ford. Containing the Public Messages, Speeches, and Statements of the President (1975) Book 1 – January 1975 – July 1975. Statement Announcing Humanitarian Assistance for Refugees in the Republic of Vietnam (March 29, 1975) (P. 406) (163). Accessed from Pennsylvania State University, Capital Campus Liberty, Middletown."

[9] Letter to the Speaker of the House and the President of the Senate transmitting proposed legislation to assist the republic of Vietnam (pp. 474-475) (181). United States Government Printing Office, "Public Papers of the Presidents of the US, Gerald R. Ford. Containing the Public Messages, Speeches, and Statements of the President (1975) Book 1 – January 1975 – July 1975. Letter to the Speaker of the

House and the President of the Senate Transmitting Proposed Legislation to Assist the Republic of Vietnam (pp. 474-475) (181) April 11, 1975. Accessed from Pennsylvania State University, Capital Campus Liberty, Middletown."

[10] Statement on the evacuation of the American mission in Phnon Penh, Cambodia (pp. 475) (182). United States Government Printing Office, "Public Papers of the Presidents of the US, Gerald R. Ford. Containing the Public Messages, Speeches, and Statements of the President (1975) Book 1 – January 1975 – July 1975. Statement on the Evacuation of the US Mission in Phnon Penh, Cambodia (pp. 475) (182) April 12, 1975. Accessed from Pennsylvania State University, Capital Campus Liberty, Middletown."

[11] With the fall of South Vietnam, Congress and President Ford repeatedly clashed over Presidential powers. Retrieve from:

http://www.geraldrfordfoundation.org/about/gerald-r-ford-biography/

(P.L 93-148)

[12] Letter to the speaker of the House and the President of the Senate reporting on the evacuation of the United States Mission in Phnom Penh, Cambodia (pp. 476-477). United States Government Printing Office, "Public Papers of the Presidents of the US, Gerald R. Ford. Containing the Public Messages, Speeches, and Statements of the President (1975) Book 1 – January 1975 – July 1975. Letter to the Speaker of the House and the President of the Senate Transmitting Proposed Legislation to Assist the Republic of Vietnam (pp. 474-475) (181) April 11, 1975. Accessed from Pennsylvania State University, Capital Campus Liberty, Middletown."

—

Chapter Sixteen

[1] Whalen, *The House and Foreign Policy*.

[2] Ibid.

[3] Briggs, *Making American Foreign Policy*, 1991.; Briggs, *Making American Foreign Policy*, 1994.

[4] Abshire, Nurnberger, and Center for Strategic and International Studies, *The Growing Power of Congress*.

[5] Zelizer, *The American Congress*.

[6] Ibid., 584.

[7] Abshire, Nurnberger, and Center for Strategic and International Studies, *The Growing Power of Congress*.

[8] Office of the Historian, Bureau of Public Affairs, "Foreign Relations of the United States, 1969–1976, Volume X, Vietnam, January 1973–July 1975 - Office of the Historian. 180. Minutes of Washington Special Actions Group Meeting."

[9] Office of the Historian, Bureau of Public Affairs, "Foreign Relations of the United States, 1969–1976, Volume X, Vietnam, January 1973–July 1975 - Office of the Historian. 181. Memorandum of Conversation."

[10] Zelizer, *The American Congress.*)

[11] Ibid.

[12] Ibid.

[13] Allison, "Conceptual Models and the Cuban Missile Crisis."

[14] Zelizer, *The American Congress.*

[15] Ibid., 593.

[16] Ibid., 599.

[17] Zelizer, *The American Congress.*

[18] Weissman, *A Culture Of Deference.*

[19] Ibid.

[20] Hackett, *The Congressional Foreign Policy Role.*

[21] With the enactment of the presidential powers act, the Unites States Congress enjoys more power over the executive branch.

[22] Robinson, *Congress and Foreign Policy-Making; a Study in Legislative Influence and Initiative.*

—

Chapter

[1] There are several online book retailers.

ABOUT THE AUTHOR

BEN WOOD JOHNSON, PH.D.

Dr. Johnson is a social observer. He is a Penn State University graduate. He holds a Doctorate in Educational Leadership and Administration; a Master's Degree in Public Administration; and a Bachelor's Degree in Criminal Justice.

Dr. Johnson also holds a Master's Degree in Political Science from Villanova University. His expertise in the field includes the following: legal theory, foreign affairs, and international conflicts. Dr. Johnson also has a background in law enforcement.

Dr. Johnson is an astute observer of human relations and human history. He writes about an array of subjects, including, but not limited to the following: politics, education, law, philosophy, legal theory, foreign relations, ethics, and administration.

To learn more about Dr. Johnson, see the *"Contact the Author"* section. You may visit his blog and official website.

You may also sign up to receive regular updates about his academic activities. Visit Dr. Johnson's cyber corner at:

www.benwoodpost.com (Official Blog)

http://www.benwoodjohnson.com (Official Website)

BIBLIOGRAPHY

Abshire, David M, Ralph D Nurnberger, and Center for Strategic and International Studies. *The Growing Power of Congress*. Washington, D.C.; Beverly Hills: Center for Strategic and International Studies, Georgetown University ; Sage Publications, 1981.

Allison, Graham T. "Conceptual Models and the Cuban Missile Crisis." *American Political Science Review* 63, no. 3 (September 1969): 689–718. doi:10.2307/1954423.

Allison, Graham T., and Philip Zelikow. *Essence of Decision: Explaining the Cuban Missile Crisis*. 2 edition. New York: Pearson, 1999.

Alpha History. "South Vietnam under Ngo Dinh Diem." *Conflict in Vietnam*. Accessed August 25, 2015. http://alphahistory.com/vietnam/south-vietnam/.

Anderson, David L. *Shadow on the White House: Presidents and the Vietnam War, 1945-1975*. University Press of Kansas, 1993.

———. , ed. *The Columbia History of the Vietnam War*. New York: Columbia University Press, 2010.

Aneja, Arpita, and Lily Rothman. "Eyewitness to the Fall of Saigon." *Time*, April 30, 2015. http://time.com/3838802/fall-of-saigon-memories/.

Associated Press. "U.S. Expected To Restore Full Relations With Vietnam | Deseret News." Accessed August 22, 2015. http://www.deseretnews.com/article/426482/US-EXPECTED-TO-RESTORE-FULL-RELATIONS-WITH-VIETNAM.html?pg=all.

Barringer, Mark. "The Anti-War Movement in the United States." *Modern American Poetry*, 1999. http://www.english.illinois.edu/maps/vietnam/antiwar.html.

Bradford, James C., ed. *A Companion to American Military History*. Blackwell Companions to American History. Chichester, U.K. ; Malden, MA: Wiley-Blackwell Pub, 2010.

Bradford, Rex. "History Matters - Vietnam Withdrawal Plans." Accessed July 5, 2015. http://history-matters.com/vietnam1963.htm.

Bresler, Robert J. "The Specter of Vietnam." *USA Today* 135, no. 2742 (March 2007). https://www.questia.com/magazine/1G1-160591309/the-specter-of-vietnam.

Briggs, Philip J. *Making American Foreign Policy : President-Congress Relations from the Second World War to the Post-Cold War Era.* 2nd ed. Rowman & Littlefield, 1994.

———. *Making American Foreign Policy: President-Congress Relations from the Second World War to Vietnam.* Lanham, Md: Univ Pr of Amer, 1991.

Brigham, Robert, K. "Battlefield Vietnam: A Brief History." Accessed August 24, 2015. http://www.pbs.org/battlefieldvietnam/history/.

Brinkerhoff, Noel, and David Wallechinsky. "How Much Does a U.S. War Cost? Ask Again in a Hundred Years." *AllGov*, March 21, 2013. http://www.allgov.com/news?news=849499.

Bullard, Natasha. "The Mercurial Role of the U.S. Media in Wartime: The Vietnam War, 1961–1975." ProQuest Dissertations Publishing, 2010.

Carpenter, Ted Galen. "A True Parallel between Vietnam, Iraq: Vitriol." *Cato Institute*, September 6, 2007. https://www.cato.org/publications/commentary/true-parallel-between-vietnam-iraq-vitriol.

Carson, Mark David. "Beyond the Solid South: Southern Members of Congress and the Vietnam War." ProQuest Dissertations Publishing, 2003.

Chapman, Steve. "Parallels Between Iraq and Vietnam." *Reason.com*, June 26, 2014. http://reason.com/archives/2014/06/26/iraq-and-the-echoes-of-vietnam.

Christopher, Jespersen, T. "Kissinger, Ford, and Congress: The Very Bitter End in Vietnam." *Pacific Historical Review*, no. 3 (2002). doi:http://dx.doi.org.ezaccess.libraries.psu.edu/10.1525/phr.2002.71.3.439.

CNN. "Vietnam War Fast Facts - CNN.com." *CNN*. Accessed July 3, 2015. http://www.cnn.com/2013/07/01/world/vietnam-war-fast-facts/index.html.

Coleman, Bradley Lynn, and Edward C. Keefer. "Foreign Relations of the United States, 1969–1976, Volume X, Vietnam, January 1973–July 1975 - Office of the Historian." Office of the Historian: Washington, 2010. Office of the Historian, Bureau of Public Affairs. https://history.state.gov/historicaldocuments/frus1969-76v10.

"Congress and the White House in the Vietnam War." *The Chronicle of Higher Education* 53, no. 9 (October 20, 2006).

CQ Press. "CQ Almanac Online Edition." Accessed August 19, 2015.

http://library.cqpress.com/cqalmanac/document.php?id=cqal75-1213988.

Daggett, Stephen. "Military Operations: Precedents for Funding Contingency Operations in Regular or in Supplemental Appropriations Bills." CRS Report for Congress. CRS Report for Congress. Congressional Research Service: The Library of Congress, June 13, 2006. https://fas.org/sgp/crs/natsec/RS22455.pdf.

Defense Casualty Analysis System. "Defense Casualty Analysis System - Conflict Casualties." Accessed August 18, 2015. https://www.dmdc.osd.mil/dcas/pages/casualties.xhtml.

———. "Defense Casualty Analysis System - Home." Accessed August 18, 2015. https://www.dmdc.osd.mil/dcas/pages/main.xhtml.

———. "Defense Casualty Analysis System - Vietnam War - Conflict Casualties." Accessed March 8, 2017. https://www.dmdc.osd.mil/dcas/pages/casualties_vietnam.xhtml.

———. "Defense Casualty Analysis System Reports - Vietnam Conflict Casualty Summary." Accessed August 18, 2015. https://www.dmdc.osd.mil/dcas/pages/report_vietnam_sum.xhtml.

DeLeon, Rudy. "Opinion: How Vietnam War Changed America." *CNN.* Accessed March 8, 2017. http://www.cnn.com/2015/06/24/opinions/deleon-vietnam-war-effects/index.html.

Embassy, U. S. "Chronology." *Http://usembassy.state.gov/chronology.html,* March 29, 2013. http://vietnam.usembassy.gov/chronology.html.

Espiritu, Yen Le. "The 'We-Win-Even-When-We-Lose' Syndrome: U.S. Press Coverage of the Twenty-Fifth Anniversary of the 'Fall of Saigon.'" *American Quarterly* 58, no. 2 (2006): 329–52. doi:10.1353/aq.2006.0042.

Feldman, Stanley. "Values, Ideology, and the Structure of Political Attitudes." In *Oxford Handbook of Political Psychology,* edited by D. O. Sears, L. Huddy, and R. Jervis, 477–508. New York, NY, US: Oxford University Press, 2003.

Felzenberg, Alvin. "Ford, Gerald R." In *Encyclopedia of U.S. Political History Volume 7,* 7:172–74, 2010.

Friedman, Jason. "Ford, Gerald (Administration of)." In *The Social History of Crime and Punishment in America : An Encyclopedia,* 2:636–37, 2012.

———. "Gerald Ford, The Mayaguez Incident, And The Post-Imperial

Presidency." *Congress & the Presidency* 37, no. 1 (January 1, 2010): 22.

Ganzel, Bill. "The Vietnam War and Rural America." *Livinghistoryfarm.org*, 2007. http://www.livinghistoryfarm.org/farminginthe50s/life_08.html.

Gorner, Peter. "Life Of A Tunnel Rat: Fighting Fear In `nam." *Tribunedigital-Chicagotribune*, June 28, 1985. http://articles.chicagotribune.com/1985-06-28/features/8502110841_1_cu-chi-american-tunnel-rats-john-penycate.

Greene, John Robert. "Essays on Gerald Ford and His Administration." *Miller Center*. Accessed July 27, 2014. https://millercenter.org/president/ford/biography/5.

Guttmann, A. "Protest against the War in Vietnam." *The Annals of the American Academy of Political and Social Science* 382, no. 1 (January 1, 1969): 56–63. doi:10.1177/000271626938200107.

Hackett, Clifford P. *The Congressional Foreign Policy Role*. Stanley Foundation, 1979.

Haley, P. Edward. *Congress and the Fall of South Vietnam and Cambodia*. Fairleigh Dickinson Univ Press, 1982.

Hallin, Daniel C. *The Uncensored War: The Media and Vietnam*. University of California Press, 1989.

Hanson, Marshal, and Scott Beaton. "Vietnam War Facts, Stats and Myths." *US Wings*. Accessed March 15, 2017. http://www.uswings.com/about-us-wings/vietnam-war-facts/.

Herman, Arthur. "Who Owns the Vietnam War?" *Commentary* 124, no. 5 (December 1, 2007): 42.

History.com. "My Lai Massacre - Vietnam War." *History.com*. Accessed March 8, 2017. http://www.history.com/topics/vietnam-war/my-lai-massacre.

History-world. "Vietnam War Statistics." Accessed March 8, 2017. http://history-world.org/vietnam_war_statistics.htm.

Hochgesang, Josh, Tracye Lawyer, and Toby Stevenson. "The Psychological Effects of the Vietnam War." Accessed August 19, 2015. https://web.stanford.edu/class/e297c/war_peace/media/hpsych.html.

Infoplease.com. "Tonkin Gulf Resolution." *Www.infoplease.com*. Accessed July 14, 2015. http://www.infoplease.com/encyclopedia/history/tonkin-gulf-resolution.html.

James, Susan Donaldson. "Suicide Rate Spikes in Vietnam Vets Who Won't Seek Help." *ABC News*, May 3, 2012. http://abcnews.go.com/Health/vietnam-vets-highest-rates-suicide-alongisde-baby-boomers/story?id=19100593.

Jespersen, T. Christopher. "Kissinger, Ford, and Congress: The Very Bitter End in Vietnam." *Pacific Historical Review* 71, no. 3 (August 1, 2002): 439–73. doi:10.1525/phr.2002.71.3.439.

———. "The Bitter End and the Lost Chance in Vietnam: Congress, the Ford Administration, and the Battle over Vietnam, 1975-76." *Diplomatic History* 24, no. 2 (April 1, 2000): 265.

Joes, Anthony James. *The War for South Viet Nam, 1954-1975*. Greenwood Publishing Group, 2001.

Jones, Steve. "American Manifest Destiny." *About.com News & Issues*, April 22, 2014. http://usforeignpolicy.about.com/od/introtoforeignpolicy/a/American-Manifest-Destiny.htm.

Jordan, Amos A., William J. Taylor Jr, Michael J. Meese, and Suzanne C. Nielsen. *American National Security*. JHU Press, 2009.

Kelly, Martin. "6 Foreign Policy Doctrines You Should Know." *About.com Education*, December 15, 2014. http://americanhistory.about.com/od/warsanddiplomacy/tp/foreign_policy_doctrines.htm.

Kenny Rogers. "Who Were U.S Presidents during the Vietnam War?" *The Vietnam War*, November 25, 2012. http://thevietnamwar.info/us-presidents-during-the-vietnam-war/.

Lardner, George Jr., and Lois Romano. "Washingtonpost.com: At Height of Vietnam, Bush Picks Guard." *The Washington Post Company*, July 28, 1999.

mapsofworld.com. "Where Is Vietnam: Vietnam Location in World Map." Accessed August 24, 2015. http://www.mapsofworld.com/vietnam/vietnam-location-map.html.

Mascaro, Tom. "The Road to War: Presidential Commitments Honored and Betrayed/Haunting Legacy: Vietnam and the American Presidency from Ford to Obama." *Journalism History* 39, no. 4 (January 1, 2014): 260.

McMahon, Robert J. "Changing Interpretations of the Vietnam War." Accessed March 8, 2017. http://www.english.illinois.edu/maps/vietnam/interpretations.htm.

Miller Center. "Gerald Ford: Impact and Legacy." *Miller Center.* Accessed March 15, 2017. https://millercenter.org/president/ford/impact-and-legacy.

National Archives. "Statistical Information about Casualties of the Vietnam War." *National Archives*, August 15, 2016. https://www.archives.gov/research/military/vietnam-war/casualty-statistics.html.

Nationsonline.org. "Viet Nam - Vietnam - Country Profile - Viêt Nam, Asia." Accessed August 24, 2015. http://www.nationsonline.org/oneworld/vietnam.htm.

O'Connor, Karen, and Larry Sabato. *American Government: Continuity and Change.* New York: Pearson Longman, 2009.

Office of the Historian, Bureau of Public Affairs. "Foreign Relations of the United States, 1969–1976, Volume X, Vietnam, January 1973–July 1975 - Historical Documents - Office of the Historian." United States Government Printing Office. *Historical Documents*, 2010. https://history.state.gov/historicaldocuments/frus1969-76v10.

————. "Foreign Relations of the United States, 1969–1976, Volume X, Vietnam, January 1973–July 1975 - Office of the Historian. 180. Minutes of Washington Special Actions Group Meeting." United States Government Printing Office. *Historical Documents*, February 27, 1975. https://history.state.gov/historicaldocuments/frus1969-76v10/d180.

————. "Foreign Relations of the United States, 1969–1976, Volume X, Vietnam, January 1973–July 1975 - Office of the Historian. 181. Memorandum of Conversation." United States Government Printing Office. *Historical Documents*, March 4, 1975. https://history.state.gov/historicaldocuments/frus1969-76v10/d181.

Office of the Historian, Bureau of Public Affairs, and United States Department of State. "James Monroe - People - Department History - Office of the Historian." Accessed March 8, 2017. https://history.state.gov/departmenthistory/people/monroe-james.

————. "U.S. Involvement in the Vietnam War: The Gulf of Tonkin and Escalation, 1964 - 1961–1968 - Milestones - Office of the Historian." Accessed July 14, 2015. https://history.state.gov/milestones/1961-1968/gulf-of-tonkin.

Olson, James Stuart. *Historical Dictionary of the 1960s.* Greenwood Publishing Group, 1999.

Ourdocuments.gov. "Our Documents - Tonkin Gulf Resolution (1964)."

Accessed July 14, 2015.
http://www.ourdocuments.gov/doc.php?flash=true&doc=98.

PBS. "An Online Companion to Vietnam: A Television History." *American Experience*, 2004. http://www.pbs.org/wgbh/amex/vietnam/.

———. "Battlefield: Vietnam (Guerrilla Tactics)." Accessed March 15, 2017. http://www.pbs.org/battlefieldvietnam/guerrilla/.

PBS, witf. "38. Gerald R. Ford . The Presidents . WGBH American Experience | PBS." *American Experience*. Accessed June 16, 2014. http://www.pbs.org/wgbh/americanexperience/features/biography/p residents-ford/.

PBS NewsHour. "Analysts Discuss Possible Iraq-Vietnam Parallels." *PBS NewsHour*, November 23, 2006. http://www.pbs.org/newshour/bb/middle_east-july-dec06-vietnam_11-23/.

———. "Chaos and the Human Costs of the Vietnam War's Final Days." *PBS NewsHour*. Accessed August 19, 2015. http://www.pbs.org/newshour/bb/chaos-human-costs-vietnam-wars-final-days/.

Pdoggbiker. "What Sets The Vietnam Veteran Apart From All Other Wars by Jack Smith." *Cherries - A Vietnam War Novel*, May 16, 2013. https://cherrieswriter.wordpress.com/2013/05/16/what-sets-the-vietnam-veteran-apart-from-all-other-wars-by-jack-smith-2/.

Peck, Grant. "Bill Clinton Visits Vietnam to Mark 20th Anniversary of Ties." *MilitaryTimes*. Accessed July 14, 2015. http://www.militarytimes.com/story/military/2015/07/02/bill-clinton-visits-vietnam-to-mark-20th-anniversary-of-ties/29621533/.

PollingReport.com. "University of Pennsylvania National Annenberg Election Survey". PollingReport.com. August 9–16, 2004. Retrieved 2007-03-30." PollingReport.com, n.d. http://www.pollingreport.com/wh04misc2.htm.

Pollingreport.com. "White House 2004: Miscellany (P. 2)." Accessed August 21, 2015. http://www.pollingreport.com/wh04misc2.htm.

Riggs, William. *Encyclopedia of the First Amendment*, 2009.

———. "Vietnam War." In *Encyclopedia of the First Amendment*, 2:1129–30, 2009.

Robertson, Andrew. *Encyclopedia of U.S. Political History*. SAGE, 2010.

Robertson, Andrew W., ed. *Encyclopedia of U.S. Political History*. Washington,

D.C: CQ Press, 2010.

Robinson, James Arthur. *Congress and Foreign Policy-Making; a Study in Legislative Influence and Initiative*. Dorsey Press, 1967.

Rottman, Gordon L. *Viet Cong Fighter*. Osprey Publishing, 2007.

Seelye, Katharine Q. "The 2004 Campaign: Military Service; Cheney's Five Draft Deferments During the Vietnam Era Emerge as a Campaign Issue." *The New York Times*, May 1, 2004. http://www.nytimes.com/2004/05/01/us/2004-campaign-military-service-cheney-s-five-draft-deferments-during-vietnam-era.html.

Stalnaker, Robert C. *A Theory of Conditionals*. Springer Netherlands, 1968. http://link.springer.com/chapter/10.1007/978-94-009-9117-0_2.

———. "A Theory of Conditionals." In *IFS*, edited by William L. Harper, Robert Stalnaker, and Glenn Pearce, 41–55. The University of Western Ontario Series in Philosophy of Science 15. Springer Netherlands, 1968. http://link.springer.com/chapter/10.1007/978-94-009-9117-0_2.

"Statistical Information about Casualties of the Vietnam War." Accessed July 15, 2015. http://www.archives.gov/research/military/vietnam-war/casualty-statistics.html.

Stephens, Frank Fletcher. "Full Text of 'The Monroe Doctrine, Its Origin, Development and Recent Interpretation.'" *Archive.org*, Social Sciences Series, 17, no. 5 (February 1916). https://www.archive.org/stream/monroedoctrineit00steprich/monroedoctrineit00steprich_djvu.txt.

Stith, Kate. "Congress' Power of the Purse." *The Yale Law Journal* 97, no. 7 (June 1, 1988): 1343–96. doi:10.2307/796443.

Stout, David. "Bush Aide Sees a Parallel Between Vietnam and Iraq." *The New York Times*, October 19, 2006. http://www.nytimes.com/2006/10/19/world/middleeast/20bushcnd.html.

Stur, Heather Marie. "Stop Comparing Iraq to the Vietnam War." Text. *The National Interest*. Accessed March 8, 2017. http://nationalinterest.org/blog/the-buzz/stop-comparing-iraq-the-vietnam-war-10788.

The American Presidency Project. "William J. Clinton: Remarks Announcing the Normalization of Diplomatic Relations With Vietnam," July 11, 1995. http://www.presidency.ucsb.edu/ws/?pid=51605.

The New York Times. "Bill Clinton's Vietnam Test." *The New York Times*, February 14, 1992, sec. Opinion. http://www.nytimes.com/1992/02/14/opinion/bill-clinton-s-vietnam-test.html.

———. "How Many Suicides by Vietnam Vets?" *The New York Times*, March 7, 1991, sec. Opinion. http://www.nytimes.com/1991/03/07/opinion/l-how-many-suicides-by-vietnam-vets-841091.html.

The Washington Times. "Biden's Draft Deferments Equal Cheney's during Vietnam War." *The Washington Times*, September 1, 2008. http://www.washingtontimes.com/news/2008/sep/1/bidens-draft-deferments-equal-cheneys-during-vietn/.

Trinity College. "Media." *Trinity College*. Accessed August 22, 2015. http://www.trincoll.edu/classes/hist300/media.htm.

Turse, Nick. *Kill Anything That Moves: The Real American War in Vietnam*. First Edition. New York: Metropolitan Books, 2013.

United States Government Printing Office. "Public Papers of the Presidents of the US, Gerald R. Ford. Containing the Public Messages, Speeches, and Statements of the President (1975) Book 1 – January 1975 – July 1975. Letter to the Speaker of the House and the President of the Senate Reporting on the Evacuation of the United States Mission in Phnom Penh, Cambodia (pp. 476-477) April 14, 1975 (183). Accessed from Pennsylvania State University, Capital Campus Liberty, Middletown." United States Government Printing Office, Washington, 1977.

———. "Public Papers of the Presidents of the US, Gerald R. Ford. Containing the Public Messages, Speeches, and Statements of the President (1975) Book 1 – January 1975 – July 1975. Letter to the Speaker of the House and the President of the Senate Transmitting Proposed Legislation to Assist the Republic of Vietnam (pp. 474-475) (181) April 11, 1975. Accessed from Pennsylvania State University, Capital Campus Liberty, Middletown." United States Government Printing Office, Washington, 1977.

———. "Public Papers of the Presidents of the US, Gerald R. Ford. Containing the Public Messages, Speeches, and Statements of the President (1975) Book 1 – January 1975 – July 1975. Statement Announcing Humanitarian Assistance for Refugees in the Republic of Vietnam (March 29, 1975) (P. 406) (163). Accessed from Pennsylvania State University, Capital Campus Liberty, Middletown." United States Government Printing Office, Washington, 1977.

————. "Public Papers of the Presidents of the US, Gerald R. Ford. Containing the Public Messages, Speeches, and Statements of the President (1975) Book 1 – January 1975 – July 1975. Statement on the Evacuation of the US Mission in Phnon Penh, Cambodia (pp. 475) (182) April 12, 1975. Accessed from Pennsylvania State University, Capital Campus Liberty, Middletown." United States Government Printing Office, Washington, 1977.

————. "Public Papers of the Presidents of the US, Gerald R. Ford. Containing the Public Messages, Speeches, and Statements of the President (1975) Book 1 – January 1975 – July 1975. The President's New Conference of April 3, 1975: Statement If the US Humanitarian Assistance to the Republic of Vietnam (pp.411-423) (166). Accessed from Pennsylvania State University, Capital Campus Liberty, Middletown." United States Government Printing Office, Washington, 1977.

Weissman, Stephen R. *A Culture Of Deference: Congress' Failure Of Leadership In Foreign Policy.* New York, NY: Basic Books, 1996.

Whalen, Charles. *The House and Foreign Policy: The Irony of Congressional Reform.* 1st New edition. Chapel Hill: The University of North Carolina Press, 1982.

Worldatlas.com. "Where Is Viet Nam? Where Is Viet Nam Located in The World? Viet Nam Map." Accessed August 24, 2015. http://www.worldatlas.com/as/vn/where-is-viet-nam.html.

Zanolli, Lauren. "What Happened When Democrats in Congress Cut Off Funding for the Vietnam War?" *History News Network,* April 13, 2007. http://historynewsnetwork.org/article/31400.

Zelizer, Julian E. "How Congress Got Us Out of Vietnam." *The American Prospect* 18, no. 3 (March 1, 2007): 30.

————. ed. *The American Congress: The Building of Democracy.* Boston: Houghton Mifflin Harcourt, 2004.

OTHER SOURCES CONSULTED

Alan Rohn. "How Much Did The Vietnam War Cost?" *The Vietnam War.* Accessed August 19, 2015. http://thevietnamwar.info/how-much-vietnam-war-cost/.

————. "Vietnam War Summary." *The Vietnam War.* Accessed July 3, 2015. http://thevietnamwar.info/vietnam-war-summary/.

American Museum of Natural History. "McCarthy Era." *American Museum of Natural History*. Accessed July 13, 2015. http://www.amnh.org/exhibitions/past-exhibitions/einstein/global-citizen/mccarthy-era.

Birney, Lawrence. "Kennedy & Merton: Raids on the Unspeakable." *THE YES FACTOR*, November 15, 2013. https://theyesfactor.wordpress.com/2013/11/14/kennedy-merton-raids-on-the-unspeakable/.

Block, Justin. "Muhammad Ali Risked It All When He Opposed The Vietnam War." *Huffington Post*, June 4, 2016, sec. Sports. http://www.huffingtonpost.com/entry/muhammad-ali-risked-it-all-when-he-opposed-the-vietnam-war_us_5751e545e4b0c3752dcda4ca.

Boorstin, Daniel J. *The Lost World of Thomas Jefferson*. 1 edition. Chicago: University Of Chicago Press, 1993.

Davidson, Roger H. *The Role of the Congressman*. Pegasus, 1969.

Democracy Now! "Military Jailing Vietnam War Resisters 40 Years After They Refused to Serve." *Democracy Now!*, March 15, 2006. http://www.democracynow.org/2006/3/15/military_jailing_vietnam_war_resisters_40.

Digital History. "Digital History." Accessed July 3, 2015. http://www.digitalhistory.uh.edu/era.cfm?eraid=18.

Douglass, James W. *JFK and the Unspeakable: Why He Died and Why It Matters*. Original edition. New York: Touchstone, 2010.
"Fs_americas_wars.pdf," n.d.

Gardner, Lloyd C., and Ted Gittinger, eds. *Vietnam: The Early Decisions*. 1st University of Texas Press ed. Austin: University of Texas Press, 1997.

Gee, Caleb. "Who Really Killed President John F. Kennedy and Why: JFK vs. the Military Industrial Complex [UPDATED]." *United States Hypocrisy*, January 3, 2014. https://ushypocrisy.com/2014/01/03/who-really-killed-president-john-f-kennedy-and-why-jfk-vs-the-military-industrial-complex/.

Greenberg, Stanley B. *The Two Americas: Our Current Political Deadlock and How to Break It*. Thomas Dunne Books, 2014.

Hall, Mitchell K., ed. *Vietnam War Era: People and Perspectives*. 1 edition. Santa Barbara, Calif: ABC-CLIO, 2009.

Hickman, Kennedy. "A Short Introduction to the Vietnam War." *About.com Education*, December 23, 2014.

http://militaryhistory.about.com/od/vietnamwar/p/VietnamBrief.htm
.

History SparkNotes. "SparkNotes: The Vietnam War (1945–1975): Summary of Events." Accessed July 3, 2015. http://www.sparknotes.com/history/american/vietnamwar/summary.html.

History.com Staff, A+E Networks. "Eisenhower Warns of Military-Industrial Complex - Jan 17, 1961." *History.com*, 2009. http://www.history.com/this-day-in-history/eisenhower-warns-of-military-industrial-complex.

"Homepage_slideshow_09_30_14.pdf," n.d.

Hoover, Margaret. *American Individualism: How a New Generation of Conservatives Can Save the Republican Party.* Reprint edition. New York; Enfield: Crown Forum, 2013.

"ils_tn_gr5_u5_c10_l4.pdf," n.d.

Jaynes, Gerald David, ed. *Encyclopedia of African American Society.* Thousand Oaks, Calif: Sage Publications, 2005.

Kumar, Kundan. *Ideology And Political System.* Discovery Publishing House, 2003.

Powell, Dennis. "Bifurcated American Politics | Newgeography.com," October 7, 2009. http://www.newgeography.com/content/001049-bifurcated-american-politics.

Saigon_helicopter.jpg (JPEG Image, 500 × 325 Pixels). Accessed July 3, 2015. http://3.bp.blogspot.com/-lkdzmuZ6uiw/U1sZSLgW9mI/AAAAAAAASBg/4gV06yjuKzE/s1600/saigon_helicopter.jpg.

Samuels, Richard J., ed. *Encyclopedia of United States National Security.* Thousand Oaks, Calif: Sage Publications, 2006.

"Sea Of Memory - A Documentary Film: Photographs." Accessed July 3, 2015. http://seaofmemorydocumentary.blogspot.com/p/photographs.html.

Sharma, Aradhana, and Akhil Gupta. *The Anthropology of the State: A Reader.* John Wiley & Sons, 2009.

Sheftall, M. *Cultural Sociology of the Middle East, Asia, & Africa : An Encyclopedia,* 2012.

Shmoop.com. "The Vietnam War Statistics." *Shmoop.com.* Accessed August

18, 2015. http://www.shmoop.com/vietnam-war/statistics.html.

Sorauf, Frank J. *Party Politics in America.* 5th edition. Boston: Little, Brown, 1984.

Spanier, John, and Joseph Nogee. *Congress, the Presidency and American Foreign Policy: Pergamon Policy Studies on International Politics.* Elsevier, 2013.

Sundquist, James L. *Dynamics of the Party System: Alignment and Realignment of Political Parties in the United States.* Brookings Institution Press, 2011.

Thinkexist.com. "Thomas Jefferson Quotes." *Thinkexist.com.* Accessed July 11, 2015. http://thinkexist.com/quotation/every_generation_needs_a_new_revo lution/225819.html.

U.S. Department of Veterans Affairs. "National Center For Veterans Analysis And Statistics Home." Accessed August 18, 2015. http://www.va.gov/vetdata/.

Vile, John R., David L. Hudson, and David A. Schultz, eds. *Encyclopedia of the First Amendment.* Washington, D.C: CQ Press, 2009.

Walker, W. E. "Congressional Resurgence and the Destabilization of US Foreign Policy." *Performer: Military Academy, West Point, NY. Sep 1988. 15p.*, September 1988, 15.

INDEX

The following is a list of important terms and keywords mentioned in the book. Please, bear in mind that this index is not exhaustive.

A

A "Senseless" war, 86

Ability, 79

Abrupt, 42, 109; abrupt departure, 42, 109

Abruptly, 7, 135; abruptly ended in the mid-1970s, 7

Abshire, David, 126

Academic, 4, 77, 81, 134, 136; Academic and governmental databases, 4; Academic approach, 136; Academic background, 134; Academic journals, 136; Academic standpoint, 77; Academic viewpoint, 81

Achieve, 33, 39, 111; Achieve that goal, 33, 39; Achieve victory, 111

Acknowledge, 62, 77, 81, 97; Acknowledge the inevitable, 62

Acting, 34, 61, 112, 118, 129; Acting as a rational actor, 129; Acting as a surrogate military force, 34; Acting as a surrogate party, 61; Acting as a unitary entity, 118; Acting on behalf of a nation, 112

Active, 7, 12, 85; Active members, 7

Activists, 17, 53, 65, 81, 102

Actor model, 105, 112, 120, 129-130

Actors, 2, 8-10, 18, 21, 61, 89, 96, 109, 114, 117-118, 131; Actors that ended the conflict, 18; Actors that participated in the decision, 21; Actors who made the ultimate decision, 89; Actors who managed the conflict, 2; Actors within the American government, 118

Additional, 9, 63, 95, 111, 120, 122, 129; Additional emergency funding, 111; Additional funding for South Vietnam and, 63; Additional funding for Vietnam, 95; Additional military aid, 120, 129; Additional military assistance, 9

Address to congress, 9

Adopt, 19, 103, 120-121; Adopt a different policy, 121; Adopt a different policy direction, 19; Adopt a different stance, 103; Advancements of North Vietnamese fighters, 87

Advisor, 62, 119, 121, 127; Advisers, 119

Affair, 66-67, 92, 112, 115, 119

Afghanistan, 58, 74, 89

Agency, 21, 106, 112; Agency funding, 21

Aggression, 27, 61

Agreement, 35, 61

Aid, 15, 18-20, 35, 61, 63, 85, 93, 104, 107, 110-111, 118, 120, 125, 127, 129, 131; Aid package, 20, 107; Aid program, 127; Aid request, 15, 18, 111; Aids, 8, 14, 31, 85; Aids and military supports, 31; Aids to the South Vietnamese, 8

Aides, 126

Airlift, 83; Airlifting embassy personnel, 86

Airplanes, 47

Ali, Muhammad, 87

Allison, Graham T., 3, 10, 65, 91, 98-99, 105, 110, 112, 114-115, 118, 125; Allison's, 105, 110, 118, 122, 128; Allison's conceptual models, 105, 110; Allison's first model, 122; Allison's models, 112, 118

Allison's approach, 128

All-out-war in Washington, 128

Ally (Political Ally), 36, 42

Ambassador, 119-120, 122, 128-129; Ambassador Dean, 119-120; Ambassador in Cambodia, 120; Ambassador to Saigon, 128; Ambassador to Vietnam, 129

Ambitious, 33; Ambitious objective, 33

America's, 32, 58-60, 78, 125; America's exit, 60; America's war, 58; American withdrawal, 105; America's own governmental actions, 78; America's problem, 32

American ambassador, (*See also*: Ambassador)

American armed forces, 123; American army, 25, 97; American personnel, 14, 85, 104, 106, 123; American beliefs, 97; American history, 25, 53, 69, 84, 97, 133; American intervention, 76

American casualties, (*See also*: Warfare)

American citizens, 123

American control, 49-50; American dominion, 133

American decision-makers, 136; American leaders, 28, 54, 68

American domestic politics, 88, 103; American politicians, 39, 63, 98; American politics, 59, 67, 75

American embassy, 11, 42, 63, 65, 83, 87, 104, 118-119; American embassy personnel, 118

American enemies, 58

American engagement, 68; American entry, 31

American evacuation, 63; American exit, 96; American helicopters, 136

American fighters, 26-28, 42, 47-49, 52, 58, 87

American fighters, 38

American foreign policy, 74, 98, 108, 112, 126; American foreign politics, 11, 67; American war, 27

American government, 30-31, 37, 41, 59, 85-86, 95, 103, 106, 120, 123; American governmental policy, 62; American officials, 3, 7, 27, 30, 39, 50, 52, 61, 74, 87, 96, 103, 107; American people, 40, 53, 66, 73, 78, 128

American heroism, 86; American military, 7, 12, 20, 25-28, 37-38, 41-42, 47-48, 51-52, 54, 58, 60-61, 75, 79, 81, 84, 86-87, 89, 93, 97, 101, 103, 123; American soldiers, 9, 25, 27-28, 38, 41, 48-49, 51-53, 58, 106; American troops, 11, 27, 37, 41, 52, 58, 61, 67, 83, 97, 102, 109-110; American warriors, 25

American idealism, 49, 55, 76; American interests, 39

American legislature, 18, 20, 96, 103-104, 127, 130; American legislators, 8

American lives, (*See also*: Death toll)

American policy, 60-61, 66, 94, 110, 119; American policymakers, 89

American presidents, 68-69

American role, 103

American scrutiny, 30

American society, 42, 53, 66, 76, 84, 134; American public, 10, 40-41, 79, 96; American values, 54

Amputation, (*See also*: Casualties - Casualty)

Analysis, 3, 41, 105-106, 110, 112, 114, 120, 135

Analysts, (*See also*: Policies)

Anger, 66, 74; Anger against the war, 74; Anger in American society, 66

Animosity against the war, 93

Anniversary of the war, 69

Anti, 79; Anti-America, 40; Anti-Communist, 35; Anti-Vietnam, 102; Antiwar, 17, 21, 31, 53, 65, 77, 79, 81, 86, 102, 128-129

Arbitrary, 126

Asian corridor, 35; Asian, 1, 29, 35; Asian continent, 1, 29

Australia, 35

B

Backbone of the manuscript, 3

Background, 88, 119, 134; Background in policymaking, 88

Backing, 19, 115

Backlashes, 79

Bait, 52

Bargain, 125; Bargaining, 114-115, 118, 125

Basic, 114, 120, 135; Basic unit of analysis, 114, 120

Battle, 14, 49, 111, 114, 128; Battlefield, 27, 36, 49, 80, 84, 120; Battleground, 12, 48-49, 58, 136

Beacon, 25; Beacon of the world, 25

Beaten, 86; Beaten in Vietnam, 86

Biden, Joseph R., 67-68

Bills, 122

Bipartisan, 57, 75, 127, 130; Bipartisanship, 130

Blame, 8, 13, 18-20, 52, 59, 61, 96, 108, 111, 129; Blaming congress, 5, 19, 59

Blog, 4, 136

Blunder (Policy Blunder), (*See also*: Policies)

Bombing, 89, 126; Bombing campaigns, 89; Bombing of Cambodia, 126

Booby, 47, 58; Booby traps, 47, 58; Booby traps/ambushes, 58

Brainchild of politicians, 54

Branches, 3, 12, 18, 66, 92, 103, 125-126, 130; Branches of government, 3, 12, 18, 66, 103, 126, 130

Bravura (American Bravura), 86

Brotherhood, 33

Brutal, 20-21, 28; Brutality, 38, 52, 60, 81; Brutality of the fighting, 38, 60; brutally massacred (Men, women, and children in My Lai), 51

Build-up (Military build-up), 37

Bureaucracy, 114; Bureaucratic, 112, 114, 116, 126, 130-131;

Bureaucratic actions, 112;
Bureaucratic activity, 116;
Bureaucratic model, 126, 130-131;
Bureaucratic political model, 114
Bush, George W., 67-68; Bush,
George H., 67-68

C

Cabinet, 10, 12, 92, 121
Cabinet members, 10, 92
Cambodia, 2, 25, 28-30, 47-48, 55, 58,
68, 79, 81, 89, 101, 119-121, 123,
126; Cambodian, 122-123;
Cambodian people, 122;
Cambodian capital of Phnom
Penh, 122
Campuses, 53, 102
Capitalism, 50
Carnage, 27, 38, 51-52
Castro, Fidel, 112
Casualties, 4, 9, 20, 27-28, 38, 47, 51,
53, 60, 85, 87, 101-102, 111;
Casualty, 41, 53
Chambers, 10, 126, 129
Chambers of congress, 10, 126
Chaotic, 11, 59, 85, 88, 104, 106
Chaotic evacuation, 11, 88
Chaotic scenery, 59
Cheney, Dick, 67-68
Chickened out, 101
Chief, 129-130; Chief of mission in
Vietnam, 129; Chief of the
American armed forces, 123
Chiefs and Indians, 116
China, 20, 29, 39, 51, 93
Chinese, 39
Church, Frank, 119

CIA (Central Intelligence Agency),
112
Cities, 47, 134
Citizen, 30, 48, 53, 66, 73, 123
City, 4, 12, 29, 83, 108; City of
Saigon, 83
Civilian, 1, 12, 26-28, 38, 42, 47, 51-
52, 54, 74, 92
Civilian and military leaders, 1, 92
Civilian death toll, 38
Civilian population, 27, 47, 51-52
Civilians, 9, 38-39, 48, 50, 86
Civilian staff members, 42
Civilization, 49
Civil unrest, 102
Civil war, 102
Clash, 1-2, 28-29, 41, 47, 58, 79, 88,
126
Cliché, 2
Clinton, Bill, 68-69
Collapse, 59, 61, 67, 110
Colonial, 30; Colonialists, 30, 33;
Colonization, 30
Colonized, (*See also*: Countries)
Combat, 1, 3, 27, 47, 85, 92, 102, 109,
120, 123
Combatants, 38
Combat-related, 53
Command, 12, 34, 123; Commander-
in-chief, 123
Commemorating the 50th
anniversary, (*See also*: Clinton, Bill)
Commit, 66-67, 73-74
Committee, 9, 14, 85, 92, 127
Communism, 7, 28, 34-35, 50, 59, 92,
109, 133; Communist, 33-36, 39,
59-60, 68-69, 76, 88, 104, 109,
121, 133
Comrades, 27

Concept, 62, 112-116

Conceptual, 3, 65, 88, 105, 110, 112; Conceptual analysis, 105; Conceptual framework, 3, 65, 88, 105; Conceptual models, 105, 110, 112

Congressional, 17, 19-20, 36, 92, 111, 126, 129-130; Constitutional, 17-18, 103, 123, 130; Constitutional authority, 18; Constitutional powers, 103; Constitutional prerogative, 17; Constitutional provisions, 130; Culprit, 4-5, 13, 17, 59

Control, 7, 12, 21, 30, 33, 35, 39, 49-50, 53, 59-60, 73, 83, 95, 108, 123, 126; Control Indochina, 59; Control Vietnamese, 39

Corridor (Asian Corridor), 35, 61

Cost, 4, 11, 20, 30, 34, 74, 98, 113; Costly, 20, 38, 42, 111, 113; Cost of the war, 20

Countries, 30, 35, 38, 50, 57-58, 73, 89, 92

Cover-up, 27-28, 51-52

Cripple 88; Crippled, 26

Crippling, 53, 69; Crippling economic embargo, 69; Crippling wounds, 53

Cuba, (*See also*: Allison, Graham T. - Allison's - Allison's models)

Cuban, 3, 65, 105, 112

Cuban missile crisis, 3, 112

Curse of Vietnam, 67

D

Daggett, Stephen, 20

D-day, 136

Dean, John Gunther, 119-120, 128

Death, 38, 50, 53, 101-102

Death and destruction, 53, 102

Deaths, 38, 53

Death toll, 38, 111

Debacle, 8, 59, 63, 86, 110, 126, 130

Decades-old conflict, 69

Decision-maker, 112, 136

Decision-making, 8, 11, 80, 88, 93, 105, 110, 126

De Facto, 39

Defense, 41, 128

Deferments, 67-68

Dehumanizing, 50

Delegate authority, 126

DeLeon, Rudy, 73

Democracy, 32, 92

Democrat, 75

Deputy Chief of mission in Vietnam, 129

Derisory, 20

Deteriorating, 120, 129

Deterioration, 97, 122-123; Deterioration of the military situation, 122; Deterioration of the situation, 123; Deterioration of the war, 97

Devastating, 42, 53, 89; Devastating and very costly, 42; Devastating effect at home, 53; Devastating military bombing campaigns, 89

Diplomatic, 1, 66, 68-69, 123; Diplomatic demarches, 66; Diplomatic efforts, 123; Diplomatic relations, 68-69; Diplomatic relationships, 69; Diplomatic vicissitudes, 1

Dire financial situation, 94

Dirksen, Everett, 127

Disagreements, 53, 57, 101

Disapproval, 75, 110, 120

Disarray, 17

Discourse, 11, 34, 57, 81, 134;
Discourse about Vietnam, 81;
Discourse in Washington, 11

Disenchanted, 53, 78

Disgruntled Americans, 38

Dissents, 102; Dissenting, 50, 75, 110

Dissident, 15; Dissidents, 14, 33, 35,
49-50, 83

Doctrine, 31, 39-40; Doctrinal, 39-40;
Doctrinal approach, 40; Doctrinal
reason, 39

Domestic, 9, 18, 30, 66-67, 75, 78-79,
88, 93, 95, 98, 102-103, 125;
Domestic dissonance, 66;
Domestic interests, 30; Domestic
issues, 75, 78-79, 125; Domestic
level, 9, 102; Domestic politics,
66-67, 88, 103; Domestic pressure,
18, 95; Domestic supports, 93

Downfall of the city, 83

Drawbacks, 18

E

Economic, 1, 14, 32, 35, 49, 69, 88,
122

Education, 130

Eisenhower, Dwight D., 35

Elderly people, 51

Embargo, 69

Embassy, 11-12, 42, 63, 65, 83, 85-87,
94, 104, 118-119

Enemies, 47, 58

Enemy, 27-28, 36, 47-48, 54, 58, 61

Enigma, 8

Equipments, 31

Era, 36, 67, 69

Escalating, 128

Executive, 8-9, 12-14, 17-18, 60, 66,
91-93, 95, 103-104, 106, 119, 123,
125-130; Commanders, 26

Exodus of people, (*See also*: Leaving -
Leaving Vietnam - Fleeing)

Expansion, 28, 34; Expansion of
communism, 28; Expansion
throughout Southeast Asia, 34

Expertise, 31, 115, 134; Expertise and
equipments, 31

Explosive, 48, 58; Explosive devices,
58

External forces, 78

Extremities (Lower), 53

F

Factor, 11, 20, 49-50, 52, 79, 110,
113, 116-117

Failure in Indochina, 1

Famous, 83, 87, 112; Famous
evacuation, 83; Famous
Muhammad Ali, 87; Famous
publication, 112

Fate, 60, 62

Faulty logics, 19

Fear at home, 9, 59

Federal government, 13, 17

Feeble, 57

Fermentation of the Vietnam War, 76

Festering at home, 3

Fiasco, 10, 19, 67, 101

Fidel Castro regime, 112

Fight, 27-28, 30, 32, 34, 37-38, 50-51,
55, 58, 81, 87, 89, 98

Fights, 39, 47-48, 58; Fights to
preserve American interests, 39

Finance, 1, 91, 94-95; Finance the war, 95; Financial, 15, 19-21, 31, 85, 93-95; Financial aid, 15, 31, 85, 93; Financial assistance, 15, 19; Financial backing, 19; Financial burden, 21; Financial cost, 20; Financial situation, 94; Financial standpoint, 20; Financial support, 19, 93-95

Firearms, 48

Firepower, 58

Firsthand accounts, 2

Foolish pride, 51

Ford, Gerald R., 9-10, 12-15, 19, 60, 62-63, 65, 85, 92, 95, 102, 104, 106-111, 118-123, 125, 127-130, 135

Foreigners, 49

Foul-ups (Mistakes), 115

Foundation, 30, 75, 92; Foundation for the American military presence, 75; Foundation of the war, 30; Foundation of this military venture, 92

Frantic, 63, 108, 135; frantic evacuation, 135; frantic move, 63, 108

Freedom, 28, 79, 92

French, 28, 30-36, 39, 41, 49-50, 88

Friedersdorf, Max, 119

Friends, 134; Friendship, 68-69

Fueled by public oppositions, 11

Fulbright, J. William, 127-128

Fundamental question, 8

Funds, 9, 94, 122; Funding, 7-9, 11, 19, 21, 41, 62-63, 85, 95, 102-103, 107, 110-111, 120, 128

Future of Vietnam, 50

G

Gadgets (Explosive), 58

Gain, 10, 68; Gaining, 9, 34; Gain steam, 10

Galvanize, 7, 87, 108; Galvanizing endorsement, 9

Gaspillage, 1

Gavin, James M., 128

General, 34, 67, 112-113, 115, 122, 125, 128

Genesis, 29; Genesis of the Vietnam War, 29; Genesis of the war, 29

Geneva (The Geneva Peace Accords), 34-35

Genuine Friendship, 69, 74; genuine friendship, 69

Geographic, 29

Geography, 29, 89

Geopolitical, 30, 34-35; Geopolitical landscape, 34; Geopolitical portal, 35; Geopolitical struggle, 30

Georgia, 127

Ghosts of Vietnam, 53

Giap, Vo Nguyen, 34

Global, 66-67, 73, 128; Global affairs, 67; Global conflicts, 66, 73; Global obligations, 128

Government, 3, 9, 11-15, 17-21, 27, 30-31, 34-35, 37, 40-43, 59-61, 63, 66-69, 73-74, 76, 79-81, 84-85, 88, 92, 94-95, 101-104, 106-109, 111-112, 114-115, 117-123, 125-126, 129-130, 133-134; About-face, 109; Government, 9, 30, 84, 86

Governmental, 3-4, 12, 59, 62, 65, 78, 83, 92, 102, 105-107, 112, 114-115, 117-118, 125-126, 131; Governmental actions, 78;

Governmental activities, 105;
Governmental affair, 92;
Governmental agency, 12, 106;
Governmental archives, 4;
Governmental branches, 126;
Governmental continuity, 107;
Governmental databases, 4;
Governmental decision, 105, 115,
117, 125; Governmental entities,
92, 106; Governmental
institutions, 102; Governmental
level, 3, 65, 83; Governmental
players, 131; Governmental policy,
62, 105, 112, 126; Governmental
politics, 105-106, 112, 114, 118
Graham, Martin A., 119
Graphic images, 102
Graveyard, 25, 27, 29, 31; Graveyard
of the American military, 25
Grim, 129
Guarantor, 36, 39; Guarantors of the
French imperialist legacy, 39
Guardian of the world, 39
Guerrilla, 27, 38, 48, 58, 87; Guerilla
fights, 58; Guerilla-type warfare,
48; Guerilla war, 87; Guerilla
warriors, 27; Guerilla weaponry,
48; Guerilla weapons, 48
Gulf, 31, 37, 75, 94; Gulf of Tonkin,
31, 37, 75, 94
GVN, 35, 42; GVN (or the
government of South Vietnam),
42; GVN or South Vietnam, 35

Hand-to-hand combats, 1
Hanoi (Capital of Vietnam), 29, 128
Hardship in Indochina, 1
Harsh economic sanctions, 88
Haste, 85; Hasty, 104, 106
Hatred for the Americans, 49
Hegemon, 32; Hegemonic, 31;
Hegemony, 93
Helicopters, 12, 47, 63, 83, 104, 123,
136
Heroism, 86
High-level cabinet members, 92
History, 1, 3, 17, 22, 25-26, 29, 45, 50,
53, 60, 69, 74, 80, 84, 86, 97, 102,
106, 133-135
Hollywood, 86
Homemade bombs, 48
Human, 1, 20, 27, 32, 42, 47-48, 52,
111, 119, 125
Human history, 1
Humanitarian, 85, 121-122, 125;
Humanitarian aid, 85;
Humanitarian assistance, 85, 122;
Humanitarian crisis, 121;
Humanitarian evacuation, 122;
Humanitarian issues, 125;
Humanitarian needs, 121
Humanity, 49
Human lives, 42, 48, 52; Human
rights, 27, 32, 125; Human shields,
47, 52; Human suffering, 20, 27
Humiliated, 39; Humiliation, 87
Hysteria, (*See also*: American
government)

H

Hackett, Clifford, 130
Hallin, Daniel, 80
Halls of history, 17, 74, 86

I

Iconic moment, 12

Ideal, 36, 49, 54-55; Idealism, 49, 55, 76
Ideological, 39-40, 49, 57, 80; Ideological framework, 39; Ideological lines, 57, 80; Ideological standpoint, 49; Ideological underpinnings, 40
Ideologically, 31, 66; ideologically driven politicians, 66
Ideologues, 60, 109
Ideology, 78; Ideologies, 49, 51, 62, 76, 133
Ill-advised, 66
Ill-conceived, 38
Illinois, 127
Illogical, 103
Imagery, 42
Images, 50, 53, 63, 79, 83, 102
Immoral, 87
Immoral war, 87
Impending doom, 12
Imperial, 35; Imperialist, 33, 39; Imperialist Brotherhood, 33; Imperialist legacy, 39
Imperial force, 35
Inability, 120
Inactions, 10, 21
Incoherent, 88, 111
Income, 26
Indecisive, 111
In-depth, 131, 136
Indians, 116
Indicator for success, 19
Indochina, 1-2, 4, 7, 9, 11-12, 19, 21, 25, 30-31, 33-34, 36-37, 39-42, 47, 55, 58-60, 65, 68, 76, 78, 81, 86, 88, 91-93, 95-98, 103-104, 109, 133-134
Indonesia, 29

Infantry, 28
Infrahuman, 50
Institutional, 10, 115
Institutions, 102, 130
Intrusion, 17
Iraq, 58, 74, 89

J

James, Susan Donaldson, 53, 119, 128, 130
Johnson, Lynden Baines, 31
Joint resolution, 75
Journalists, 79
Journals, 136
Jungle, 2, 25, 28, 38, 48-49, 58, 79, 81, 84, 87, 89, 101; Jungle battles, 79; Jungle fighting, 48; Jungle-like, 47, 58; Jungles of Cambodia, 2, 48; Jungles of Laos, 58, 89, 101; Jungle warriors, 25

K

Kennan, George F., 128
Kennedy, John F., 102
Kerry, John F., 68
Khmer Republic, 122; Khmers, 120
Kinds, 48, 52, 54, 58, 128; Kind of motivation, 54; Kind of war, 52; Kind of warfare, 48, 58; Kinds of explosive, 58; Kinds of issues, 128
Kissinger, Henry, (*See also*: Advisor)
Korean War, 53

L

Laboratory, 58

Landmines, 47

Lao PDR, 29; Lao, 29; Lao people's democratic republic, 29; Laos, 2, 25, 28, 30, 47-48, 55, 58, 81, 89, 101

Law enforcement, 53

Lawmakers, 126

Layperson, 88

Leader, 1, 28, 33, 50, 54, 68, 74, 86, 92-93, 114-115, 121, 126-127

Leave, 3, 42, 83-84, 86-87, 96-98, 108-109, 122; Leave Vietnam, 3, 42, 86-87, 96-98

Leaving, 83, 85, 87, 89, 95, 107; Leaving the region, 107; Leaving Vietnam, 83, 85, 87, 89, 95; Fleeing, 42, 108

Legacy, 10, 14, 39

Legal foundation, 75

Legislation, 75, 128

Legislative, 9-10, 13, 17-19, 59, 66, 92, 103, 109, 120, 125, 128-130; Legislative body, 128; Legislative branch, 9-10, 13, 17, 19, 59, 103, 109, 120, 125, 129; Legislative setting, 10

Legislature, 3, 9, 13, 17-18, 20, 62, 76, 96, 103-104, 107, 126-127, 129-130; Legislators, 8, 13, 15, 85, 93, 111, 121, 128

Lend, 33, 36

Lessons, 130; Lesson in Vietnam, 89

Lethal, 26, 58

Liberals, 57, 80

Litmus test, 65, 67-69

Long-term, 57, 59, 61, 63, 74, 101; Long-term effects from the Vietnam War, 74; Long-term effects of the war, 57, 59, 61, 63, 101

Lyndon, Baines Johnson, 31, 36, 75, 92

M

Machine, 25, 27

Madness, 1

Malaise, 26

Malaysia, 29

Mandate, 36, 76

Maneuver, 14, 127

Manifest destiny, 39

Mansfield, Mike, 127

Marine, 12, 63, 83, 104, 123; Marine helicopters, 12, 63, 83, 104

Massacre (My Lai), 51-52; Massacred, 51; Massacred men, women, children, 51

McGee, Gale, 127

Mechanism, 10, 78, 80, 88, 91, 110, 112, 135-136

Media, 79-81, 96, 111, 121; Ability to report the war, 79

Memorandum, 121, 127

Message, 13, 62-63, 93, 119, 129

Metric, 11

MIA (Missing in Action) or Prisoner of War (POW), 37

Military-industrial complex, 74

Minority leader, 127

Miscalculated, 122

Misconducts, 27

Mississippi, 127

Mistake, 1, 26

Models, 2-4, 10, 65, 91, 105-106, 110, 112, 117-119, 121, 123, 129

Modern warfare, 1

Momentum, 87

Money, 7, 19, 86, 94; Money problem, 7

Monolithic group, 114, 126

Montana, 127

Morse, Wayne, 128

Mortal danger, 120

Multinational, 57

Mundt, Karl E., 127

Mystery, 1, 8, 11, 80, 88

Myth of presidential superiority, 130

N

Naïve, 78

National, 50, 53, 67, 112-114, 120-121, 123, 129

Nationalism, 50

Nationalist, 34

Nations, 1, 35, 39, 69, 73, 93, 112, 121, 125

NATO or the United Nations, 73

Naval, 28, 31, 121; Naval power, 28; Naval ship, 31; Naval transport, 121

News, 37, 118, 121; Newscasts, 53, 111; Newspapers, 81

New York Times, 53

New Zealand, 35

Night, 48; Nightclubs, 48

Nightmare, 111

Nixon, Richard, 40, 60-63, 76, 102, 107, 120, 127

Nixon's request to increase military aid, 111

Nixon Administration, 107, 111, 119; Nixon's foreign policies, 119

Non-combatants, 38

Nonconformist, 49

Non-veterans, 26

Nuclear, 113

Nuke, 116

Nurnberger, Ralph, 126

O

Obama, Barack, 68-69

Objectification, 49-50; Objectification of fighters, 49; Objectification of the Vietnamese, 50; Photos taken during the war, 50

Offensive, 97, 122

One-sided, 54, 88

Opposition, 9, 11, 85, 128; Oppositions, 9-11

Overestimate, 122

Overlook, 11, 75, 104

Overreach, 111

Overseas, 92-93

P

Package, 20, 107; Packaged their messages, 93

Pakistan, 35

Paris, 61; Paris accord, 61; Paris agreement, 61

Parochial priorities, 114, 127

Patriotism, 57, 81

Patrolling the gulf of Tonkin, 31

PDR, 29

Peace, 34, 76, 92

Phnom Penh, 122

Polarizing, 73

Police, 53-54

Policies, 1, 10-11, 34, 54, 66, 87, 105, 110, 112, 119, 130; Policy advisers, 62, 119; Policy analysts, 11; Policy approach, 39, 98, 107; Policy decision, 3, 103-104, 106; Policy initiative, 18-19, 62, 66, 73-74, 93, 98, 109, 111, 126, 128, 130; Policy venture, 102, 133, 135; Policy outcomes, 131; Policy reversal, 7, 108; Policy exploration, 4; Policy plans, 126; Policy paradigm, 112; Policy blunder, 1; Policy standpoint, 11, 80, 88, 107, 134; Policy change, 63, 65; Policy choice, 60, 94, 103, 109, 126; Policy credentials, 68; Policy framework, 11, 31, 65, 93; Policy issues, 17, 126; Policy options, 127, 129; Policy ramifications, 136; Policymakers, 2-3, 54, 57, 59-61, 78, 89, 94, 96, 103, 106, 111, 114, 125; Policymaking, 65-66, 78, 88, 106, 112, 119, 125, 127, 129-131, 135; Policy matters, 18; Policy mechanism, 10, 91, 112, 136; Policy rationale, 2-4, 63, 89, 95, 103, 105, 107, 131, 135; Policy reason, 62, 83, 91, 96

Policy advisor, (*See also*: Policies - Policy advisers)

Politicians, 10-11, 39-40, 42, 54, 57, 63, 66-68, 74, 77, 80, 87, 98, 103

Populi, 78

Portal, 35

POW, 37

Presidents, 67-69, 76, 92, 111, 126; Presidential, 68, 107, 126, 130; Presidential campaign, 68; Presidential domination, 130; Presidential powers, 126; Presidential superiority, 130; Presidential vacancy, 107

Prize, 11, 68, 133

Propaganda, 27, 103

Prophecy, 15

Protest, 38, 53, 86, 102

Proxy, 40, 98

Psychological, 48, 74

Pundits, 86

Punitive war, 39, 58

Q

Qualms in Vietnam, 27

Quandary, 109

Quasi certain, (*See also*: Cover-up)

Quest, 8

Questions, 12-13, 18, 29, 59, 67, 85, 88, 95-96, 104, 114, 128

Quick summary, 136

Quintessence, 12

R

Radar, 41

Radical, 30

Rally, 129

Random affair, 115

Rational-actor, 105, 112, 120, 129-130; Rational-actor framework, 120; Rational-actor model, 105, 112, 120, 129-130

Reagan, Ronald, 68

Rebellion, 33

Rebels, 32, 50

Recalcitrant anti-war activists, 102

Relations, 68-69, 127, 130; Anniversary, (*See also*: Clinton, Bill)

Relationship, 69, 114, 130

Reminiscent, 58

Remote, 48, 51

Repercussion, 25, 34, 74

Republic, 29, 35, 122

Republican, 57, 75-76, 111, 127, 130

Resilience, 122

Resist, 28, 122

Resistance, 1, 25, 102

Resources, 1, 21, 30, 111, 121, 128

Response, 35, 112, 121

Responsibilities, 61-62, 114, 123

Retaliate, 76; Retaliation, 27

Revolutionary war, 30, 33

Revolutions, 59

Rigidity of the environment, 54

Rituals (American policy-making rituals), 66

Roadblock, 95

Rogue (Soldiers), 27-28

Rooftop, (*See also*: Marine - Marine helicopters)

Ruling class, 30

Run, 63, 86, 109; Running away, 42

Rush decision, 89

Rusk, Dean, 128

Russell, Richard, 127

Russia (former Soviet Union), 39

Ruthless, 48

S

Sabotage, 103

Sabotaged, 111

Saigon, 4, 11-13, 29, 42, 63, 65, 83, 87-88, 93, 104, 106, 108, 110, 118, 128, 135-136

Sanctions, 88

Sanctity of South Vietnam, (*See also*: Ford, Gerald R.)

Scapegoat, 35

Scar, 66

Scenario, 25, 34, 58, 83, 121

Scene, 104, 120; Scenery, 59

Schlesinger, James, 119

Scientific approach, 2, 14, 98, 101, 103, 105, 107

Scientist (Political Scientists), 105

Scowcroft, Brent, 119

Scrambling, 9, 12, 136

Screens, 79, 102

Scuffle, 36, 47, 74, 133

SEATO, 34-35; SEATO accord, 34

Security, 76, 113, 129

Self-determination, 30, 50

Self-fulfilling, 15

Self-inflicted, 53, 60

Senate, 9-10, 127-128

Senator, 67-68, 128

Senators, 128

Sensational, 67

Setback, 25, 34, 120, 133

Sheer, 38, 52, 81, 102; Sheer brutality, 38, 52; Sheer level of brutality, 81; Sheer number of American casualties, 102

Shields (human shields), 47, 52

Shortcomings, 77

Shortsighted, 96

Showcase, 81

Skirmishes, 29, 32-33, 41, 53, 66-67, 106

Sneaky attacks, 48

Snub military services, 67

So-called, 34, 61, 67; So-called "domino effect", 34; So-called "Vietnamization", 61

Socialist revolutions, 59

Soldiers, 9, 25, 27-28, 38, 41, 48-49, 51-53, 58, 106

Southeast, 11, 28-29, 31, 34-35, 39-
    40, 59, 62, 69, 76, 93, 128;
    Southeast Asia, 11, 28-29, 31, 34-
    35, 39-40, 59, 62, 69, 76, 93, 128
Southern, 19, 36, 95, 106, 108;
    Southern regions, 106; Southern
    Vietnamese, 36, 106
Soviet Union (Now Russia), 39, 51,
    92-93, 113
Steady-state choice, 113
Stennis, John, 127
Street, 53, 58, 102
Student deferments, 67
Subjects, 55
Subjugated, 30, 50, 55
Suffer, 66
Suffering, 20, 27-28, 51, 86
Suicide, 53-54; Suicide-related, 53
Superiority, 38, 130; Superior military
    advantages, 28; Superior military
    power, 28
Supermarkets, 48
Support, 8, 19, 31, 36, 40, 53, 57-58,
    63, 73, 75, 77, 84-85, 87, 93-95,
    98, 102-103, 106, 108, 110, 120-
    121, 123, 127, 129-130; Backing of
    the United States, 19
Supranational, 73
Surrogate, 34, 40-41, 61, 98;
    Surrogate army, 98; Surrogate
    military, 34, 41; Surrogate party,
    61; Surrogate war, 40-41
Sway dissidents, 14
Switzerland, 34
Sworn-in, 107
Sympathizers, 109
Syndrome, 105

T

Tableau, 4, 30
Tactic, 48, 58
Tactical air, 123
Tantrum, 26
Taylor, Maxwell, 128
Techniques, 58
Technologies, 28
Telegram, 119-120
Televised, 81, 128
Television, 53, 79, 102; Television
    broadcasts, 53; Television screens,
    79, 102
Tension, 69
Terrains, 48
Territory, 7, 14, 39
Texas, 127
Thailand, 29, 35
Theoretical, 2, 105; Theoretical
    explanations, 105; Theoretical
    framework, 2; Theoretical tool,
    105
Theory, 31, 41, 60; Theories, 8, 105
Thieu, Nguyen Van, 59, 61, 119, 122,
    128
Tonkin, 31, 36-37, 75-76, 94; Tonkin
    attack, 31, 37; Tonkin incident, 31,
    36-37, 94; Tonkin resolution, 75-
    76
Topography of the land, 48
Touchy subject, 134
Tower, John, 127
Toxic political hodgepodge, 9
Traditional fights, 39
Tragic, 1, 27
Trauma, 54
Treacherous, 7, 9, 11-13, 15
Triumphs, 1

Truce, 61

Truman, Harry, 31, 33-34, 40, 88, 92

Tunnels, 48

Turmoil, 107

Turse, Nick, 27; Kill Anything That Moves, (*See also*: Cover-up)

Two-dimensional war, 62

Two-thirds of the country, 110

Typical, 135

U

Ulterior motive, 11

Unacceptable, 50

Unachievable, 54

Unambiguous, 12

Unanimous, 60

Unbearable embarrassment, 128

Unconditional, 33, 95

Uncontrollable, 127

Undermine, 4, 35

Underpinnings of the American presence, 40

Undertaken, 2, 66, 78

Unification, 57, 78

Unified mission, 54

Uniformed approach, 86

Unilateral decision, 122

Unions, 102

Unitary, 112, 114, 117-118, 120-121, 131; Unitary actor, 117; Unitary agent, 121; Unitary decision-maker, 112; Unitary entity, 118; Unitary level, 131; Unitary nation, 114; Unitary rational nation, 120

Unorthodox, 47

Unpopular, 38, 40, 53, 102, 109, 121, 128

Unpopularity of the war, 102

Unusual settings, 47

Upheaval, 66

Urban, 47, 58; urban areas, 47; urban fights, 58

Urban-style, 49, 58; Urban-style battles, 49; Urban-style warfare, 58

Urgency, 115

Utility function, 112

V

Vacancy, 107

Vacuum, 109

Vague piece of legislation, 76

Validate the war, 38

Valuable, 42, 89

Valuable ally, 42

Valuable lesson, 89

Value, 4, 20, 54, 77, 113

Veterans, 26, 53, 68, 82

Victims, 27, 51

Victorious, 133

Victory, 7, 13, 20, 54, 75, 84, 102-103, 111

Vietcong, 51-52, 84-85; Vietcong army, 52, 85; Vietcong fighters, 51; Vietcong forces, 84

Vietnamization, 61

Vietnam-related, 53

Village, 48, 51-52

Violence, 128

Visceral, 31, 102

Voice, 50, 75, 78; Voiced, 75, 120; Voiced their disapproval of the war, 120; Voiced their staunch disapproval, 75

Voices, 15, 35, 75, 110; Voices against the war, 75; Voices in congress, 15

Voix, 78; Voix du people, 78; Vox, 78; Vox populi, 78
Vowed, 109

W

Wage a war, 33
Walls, 83, 95
War-exit, 91, 93, 95, 97
Warfare, 1, 28, 38, 48, 53, 58, 102, 126
War-fighting strategies, 58
War-making policies, 10
Warmongers, (*See also*: Military-industrial complex)
Warriors, 25, 27
Wartime, 111, 130
Washington, 2, 7, 9-14, 18-19, 21, 57, 59, 61-63, 65, 74, 84, 96-97, 106-107, 110, 120, 127-129, 136
Weakening the American government, 61
Weaponry, 48, 58
Weapons, 48, 52, 113
Wee hours, 12
Weissman, Stephen, 129
Well-being, 48
Well-calculated strategy, 63, 121
Well-orchestrated propaganda, 27
West, 29
We-Win-Even-When-We-Lose, 105
White house, 62, 95
Withdrawal, 3-4, 8-12, 63, 66, 75, 79, 83, 94, 96-99, 103, 105-107, 110-112, 118-119, 122, 125, 135-136; Withdrawal day, 12; Withdrawal decision, 3-4, 8-12, 63, 66, 75, 94, 96-97, 99, 103, 105-106, 110, 112,

122; Withdrawal policy, 4, 10, 106, 110, 119, 125
Wolfgang, Lehmann J., 119
Women, 47, 51, 101-102; Women and children, 47
Won, 20, 63, 87, 105, 133-134
Won the conflict, 134; Won the war, 20, 63, 87, 133; Won the war, 133; Won the war itself, 133; Won the war militarily, 87
Worldview, 4, 34, 39, 54, 76, 97
Worldwide, 58
Worldwide supports, 58
Would-be-American-foes, 58
Wyoming, 127

Y

Years of hand-to-hand combats, 1
Yen Le, Espiritu, 105
Young, 49, 52-53, 101-102
Youth resistance, 102

Z

Zelizer, Julian, 128
Zone (Combat Zone), 47, 123

DEAR READER

Thank you for purchasing this book.

If you enjoyed this book or found it useful, I would be eternally grateful if you were to take the time and post a short review about your reading experience on any preferred platform.

Your support will make a big difference in helping me improve my intellectual contribution to the world. Your feedback will also help me improve the content quality in this book. I read all the reviews personally. With your help, I hope to make this book better suitable for a wonderful reading experience.

I look forward to having you as a loyal reader and reviewer. Thank you so much for your support.

Cordially,
BWJ

CONTACT THE AUTHOR

Find Ben Wood on Social Media and the Web
Ben Wood Twitter handle is @benwoodpost
Ben Wood Facebook page @benwoodpost
Ben Wood official blogs at: www.benwoodpost.com
Ben Wood official website: www.benwoodjohnson.com
Ben Wood CV website: www.benwoodjohnsoncv.com

MAILING/POSTAL INFO:

PO Box 214
Middletown, PA
Zip: 17057

PHONE:

Tel: 717-510-3420

ELECTRONIC ADDRESS:

E-mail: benwoodpost@gmail.com

Other Works

Sartrean Ethics: A Defense of Jean-Paul Sartre As A Moral Philosopher

This text examines the nature of the works Sartre compiled about ethics. It explores some of the arguments that are often offered against the role Sartre played in the ethical genre. It seeks to demonstrate that Sartre was a moral philosopher by referencing the works of several scholars in the field.

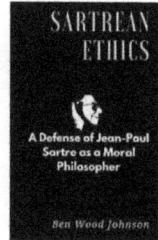

Jean-Paul Sartre and Morality: A Legacy Under Attack

The Sartrean legacy in moral philosophy is under siege. While Jean-Paul Sartre is regarded as a well-accomplished writer in philosophy, novel, playwright, and biography, just to name a few, many are convinced that ethics was not his strongest suit. His approach to morality is often rebuked vociferously.

Sartre Lives On

This short opus explores the debate regarding the moral philosophy of Jean-Paul Sartre. It examines the many issues that are often levied against this brilliant thinker. This text is only a preamble to several other works the author compiled on the subject. It does not assess the ramifications of misguided views towards the Sartrean legacy.

Left Blank

Left Blank

Left Blank